The Persians

THE SEAFARERS
WORLD WAR II
THE GOOD COOK
THE TIME-LIFE ENCYCLOPAEDIA
OF GARDENING
HUMAN BEHAVIOUR
THE GREAT CITIES
THE ART OF SEWING
THE OLD WEST
THE WORLD'S WILD PLACES
THE EMERGENCE OF MAN
LIFE LIBRARY OF PHOTOGRAPHY
THIS FABULOUS CENTURY
TIME-LIFE LIBRARY OF ART
FOODS OF THE WORLD
GREAT AGES OF MAN
LIFE SCIENCE LIBRARY
LIFE NATURE LIBRARY
YOUNG READERS LIBRARY
LIFE WORLD LIBRARY
THE TIME-LIFE BOOK OF BOATING
TECHNIQUES OF PHOTOGRAPHY
LIFE AT WAR
LIFE GOES TO THE MOVIES
BEST OF LIFE

The Emergence of Man

The Persians

by Jim Hicks
and the Editors
of Time-Life Books

Time-Life International
(Nederland) B.V.

The Author: JIM HICKS, formerly on the staff of LIFE, has travelled extensively throughout the Middle East and for many years has nourished an interest in the ancient civilizations of that area. Now a freelance writer, Hicks is the author of *The Empire Builders*, a previous volume in The Emergence of Man series, and has written numerous articles, for which he has twice been the recipient of reporting awards from The National Headliners Club.

The Consultants: ROGER MOOREY is a curator of the Ashmolean Museum at Oxford University responsible for the collection of Middle Eastern and Egyptian antiquities. He has participated in archaeological excavations at Jerusalem, and his published works include three volumes on his speciality, the metalwork of ancient Iran. EDITH PORADA holds the distinguished Arthur Lehman professorship at Columbia University and is on the faculty of art history and archaeology. In her researches she has concentrated on the cultural artifacts of the Middle East and the light they shed on religious and social development in the ancient world. She has contributed numerous articles to scholarly journals in her field and is author of *The Art of Ancient Iran*. DALE BISHOP, a member of the anthropology department at Columbia and a specialist in Iranian languages and literature, assisted with the preparation of Chapter Four of this book.

The Cover: Near Persepolis, a Persian treasury official, dressed in the robes of the royal court and wearing a typical fluted felt hat, inspects the work of a Greek artisan from Persian-held Ionia. The sculptor is fashioning a six-foot-high limestone statue of a bull that, when finished, will serve as the capital for a 60-foot-high structural column at the palace complex. To achieve perspective, another official stands back and assesses the proportions of the carving. The human figures in this Fifth Century B.C. scene were painted by artist Michael A. Hampshire on a photograph of the statue taken at present-day Persepolis.

ISBN 7054 0126 X

Contents

Introduction

The Geologic Time Scale

For many years experts have argued about the dates to be assigned to the eras, periods and epochs of the geologic time scale. The scale generally accepted for many years has been founded on one that was devised by J. Laurence Kulp of Columbia University. But more recently a scale compiled for the Elsevier Scientific Publishing Company has gained wide acceptance. The scale used here in this book is an updated Kulp scale; its relationship to the Elsevier scale can be seen below.

	DATE MILLIONS OF YEARS AGO	
	Kulp Scale	Elsevier Scale
Paleozoic Era		
Cambrian Period	600	570
Ordovician Period	500	500
Silurian Period	440	435
Devonian Period	400	395
Carboniferous Period		
Mississippian Epoch	350	345
Pennsylvanian Epoch	325	310
Permian Period	270	280
Mesozoic Era		
Triassic Period	225	230
Jurassic Period	180	195
Cretaceous Period	135	141
Cenozoic Era		
Tertiary Period		
Paleocene Epoch	70	65
Eocene Epoch	60	55
Oligocene Epoch	40	35
Miocene Epoch	25	22.5
Pliocene Epoch	10	5
Quaternary Period		
Pleistocene Epoch	2	1.8

In 1971 the Shah of Iran celebrated the 2,500th anniversary of the founding of the Persian Empire by Cyrus the Great. Among the millions of people throughout the world who saw on television the splendid tented camp erected for the ceremonies at Persepolis, only a relative handful would have truly appreciated the achievements of the Achaemenid monarchy that Cyrus established. "The laws of the Medes and Persians that altereth not" became proverbial through the Biblical Book of Daniel, but the Persians' other remarkable works have been obscured by the biased interpretations of the Greek and Roman historians who provide so much of the surviving information.

In 330 B.C. the triumphant young Alexander the Great of Macedonia set fire to Persepolis—possibly in a moment of drunken frenzy. In doing so, he marked for all time, even more dramatically than he knew, the end of the greatest empire before that of Rome. In all the centuries since, wind, rain and the depredations of men could not completely obliterate the ruins of Persepolis, but the Biblical Book of Esther and Classical accounts masked Persia's glory behind legends of its profligacy and brutality.

The ambitions, achievements and failures of the great Persian kings began to re-emerge only after 1931, when archaeologists started to excavate Persepolis. Under the rubble there and in subsequent digs at other sites of the realm was compelling evidence that, behind its traditional malevolent image, the ancient Persian Empire had worn a much more attractive and benign face.

The efforts of modern scholars have revealed that the Book of Esther's well-told tale of harem intrigue and massacres at the court of King Xerxes is real enough. However, by sifting speculation through the screens provided by archaeological data and textual sources outside the Bible, it has become evident that disastrous feuding within the Persian royal family and vicious struggles for power at court and in the provinces slowly but surely dissipated the vast domain created by Cyrus; the empire that Alexander crushed had long been dying. By emphasizing the period of decline, the often melodramatic story of Persia's fall served to conceal its finest hours.

At their best the Persians were superb administrators, were tolerant of local religious beliefs and had impressively sensitive sacred traditions of their own. They loved gardens and paid great attention to the conservation of nature; from their term for "park" we have inherited the evocative word "paradise". The enormous wealth of the king and the aristocracy stimulated high standards of workmanship among metalsmiths and jewellers, and also inspired craftsmen working with more perishable materials. One isolated piece of testimony to their skill—the oldest Persian carpet—has survived only because it was deep-frozen in the grave of a Siberian chieftain, whom it reached through one of the tentacles of trade that extended from the Persian homeland across the vast expanses of Asia.

As a schoolboy, I first encountered the ancient Persians in the vivid narratives written by the Greek chroniclers Herodotus and Xenophon. It is through them that some of the best historical material in this volume has survived. In the Fifth Century B.C., Herodotus travelled deep into the Persian Empire and recorded what he saw and heard. At the very end of the same century, Xenophon served as a mercenary in the army of a Persian provincial governor who was trying vainly to take the crown from his own brother, King Artaxerxes II.

When, as an adult, I first visited Babylon, and then Susa, Persepolis and Pasargadae, I was more grateful to these two Greek writers than I had ever imagined possible. Without their comments, I know I could have found it easy to dismiss these gaunt, eroded ruins as forlorn and dull. But as I remembered the clear descriptions—so skilfully recorded by these historians—of men, places and events, spiced with court and army gossip, the ruins came alive.

On the pages that follow, the testimony of these incomparable human witnesses has been combined with the cumulative findings of modern archaeological research. The result evokes a people no less remarkable than the better-known ancient Egyptians and Babylonians, whom the Persians conquered, and equally as interesting as the Greeks, who conquered the Persians and learned so much from them and their former vassals in the process.

P. R. S. Moorey
Ashmolean Museum, Oxford University

Chapter One: The Giant Imperial Machine

When the ruler of an old and wealthy kingdom in Asia Minor was confidently preparing for war against Persia around 547 B.C., a wise man came to the court to urge the king to reconsider, arguing that the risks of such a venture offset the advantages. "My lord, you are preparing to fight against men who dress in leather—both breeches and everything else. So rough is their country that they eat as much as they have, never as much as they want. They drink no wine but only water. They have no good things at all, not even figs for dessert. Now if you conquer this people, what will you get from them, seeing they have nothing for you to take? And if they conquer you, think how many good things you will lose."

Such words of caution, in the king's view, were foolish. These Persians were hardly even a nation. They had only recently given up a nomadic life on the steppes to settle in a small, rugged and inhospitable region of southwest Asia, vassals first to one and then another of their long-established and more powerful neighbours. But as the unheeding ruler bent on war with Persia was to discover—at the cost of his realm and his life—this meagre beginning did not deter the Persians, whose explosive rise to power swept aside all opposition.

Starting in 559 B.C., the Persians needed only about 30 years to burst from obscurity and create the first world empire. In that time span—little more than a generation—people from Greece to Ethiopia,

Adorned with the curls characteristic of Achaemenid royalty, this head of a youth bears a crown that resembles the battlements at the fabled city of Persepolis, where the sculpture was found. Though less than three inches high, the head projects the stolid self-assurance of all imperial Persian portraits. It is made of Egyptian blue, a glasslike material.

from Libya to India came to regard the monarch on the throne of Persia as the only king who mattered. Thus, the Persians were the first people to realize an ancient dream: the large-scale establishment, throughout the entire Middle East, of a powerful community administered under a common language —in this instance, Aramaic—and under a single ruler. The resulting empire, nearly two million square miles in extent, was populated by around 10 million people.

The prime movers of this stunning assertion of centralized power were the Achaemenids—the Persian ruling family. Exploiting their own uncommonly wise statesmanship and managerial excellence, they ushered their newly unified world into an era of increasing trade and improving living standards such as mankind had never before experienced. For almost 200 years under the Achaemenids' protection, goods and people and ideas crossed old boundaries with relative ease, and in the process transformed such great cities of the empire of Babylon into truly cosmopolitan centres.

Conquest was the spearhead of Persian expansion. But for all the military prowess at their command, the Achaemenids could not have held together their vast, heterogeneous domains by force alone. "The spear of a Persian man has gone forth far," wrote one of the great kings, Darius. But much of the strength behind that spear was drawn from a constantly extended and improved system of communications, a sophisticated governmental structure and, above all, a surprising tolerance for the laws and traditions of their subject peoples; this indulgence was an enormous factor, socially and psychologically, in securing loyalty and obedience from the vanquished. Even in the matter of religion the Persians were permissive.

Early in their imperial history they came to have a vital national faith of their own, based on a pantheon headed by the god Ahuramazda, whom they deemed to be the creator of heaven, earth and man. But the Persians made no attempt to impose their beliefs elsewhere; instead, they lent positive encouragement to the religious tenets of those they ruled, on the enlightened theory that the conquered populations would return the favour with a degree of support.

The Persians' political sagacity was not to be matched by cultural achievements of their own. Their educational ideals were limited: "To ride a horse, to draw a bow, and to speak the truth." Originality in arts and sciences they left largely to others; they were content to appropriate the best accomplishments of their vassals and recast them in their own image. Archaeologists examining the ruins of the Persians' imperial residence at Parsa (better known by its Greek name, Persepolis) can trace various stylistic elements of its design to the Babylonians, Assyrians, Egyptians and Greeks—all of whom were Persian subject peoples. But the aura of majesty the Achaemenids achieved in constructing their huge lofty-columned halls does reflect their own soaring ambition and pride.

Pride was an essential element in the ancient Persian character: pride in their king, in their homeland, in the essential simplicity with which they viewed their lives. By tradition no Persian ever prayed for himself, only for his king and country. And once, when a nobleman suggested to the first imperial Persian ruler, Cyrus the Great, that he move the court from Pasargadae—where the climate was difficult—to a site in his domain where the weather was more pleasant, the king answered that he would stay where

A Persian Chronology

2000-1800 B.C.
Beginning of Aryan (Iranian) migration from plains of southern Russia into Middle East.

c. 2000-550 B.C.
Assyria, Media, Babylonia and Lydia are dominant powers in Middle East.

628 B.C.
Birth of Zoroaster, religious prophet.

c. 575 B.C.
Birth of Cyrus the Great.

559 B.C.
Cyrus assumes throne of Anshan (western Persia) and begins subjugation of all Persia.

547 B.C.
Cyrus defeats King Croesus of Lydia.

539 B.C.
Babylonia falls to Cyrus; release of Israelite captives.

530-525 B.C.
Death of Cyrus and accession of Cambyses II.

522-521 B.C.
Darius assumes throne amid turmoil throughout empire.

c. 520 B.C.
Introduction of standardized imperial coinage; reorganization and extension of Royal Road system.

513-512 B.C.
First Asian invasion of Europe; Persians conquer Thrace and Macedonia.

490 B.C.
Battle of Marathon; Greeks defeat Persians.

486 B.C.
Coronation of Xerxes, son of Darius.

480-479 B.C.
Persians defeated by Greeks in battles at Thermopylae, Salamis, Plataea and Mycale; era of Persian expansion ended.

465-330 B.C.
Reigns of Artaxerxes I to Darius III; decline of Persian vigour and influence; economic, military and political decay.

336 B.C.
Rise to power of Alexander the Great of Macedonia.

330 B.C.
Alexander destroys Persian Empire; Persepolis burned.

301 B.C.
Seleucus, one of ablest Macedonian commanders, founds Seleucid Dynasty by gaining control of Iran, Mesopotamia, northern Syria and much of Asia Minor.

c. 171 B.C.
Mithridates I, King of Parthians, establishes an empire reaching from Babylonia to Bactria.

224 A.D.
Ardashir I defeats Parthians and founds Sasanian Empire.

260 A.D.
Shapur I, Ardashir's son, captures Roman emperor Valerian at Battle of Edessa.

642 A.D.
Fall of Sasanian Empire after defeat by Arabs at Nihavend.

he was. "Soft lands," he said, "breed soft men." The Persians considered everything about their native land to be superior, even the water. Cyrus is reported to have drunk only from the river Choaspes near Pasargadae; he carried supplies from it in silver jugs on his far-flung campaigns.

The pride and the prayers worked as long as Persia was blessed with strong leaders. But many years before its final collapse around 330 B.C., the empire had begun to evidence some of the afflictions suffered by more recent superpowers—among them violent internal struggles, corruption and raging inflation.

Modern scholars have had to assemble knowledge of the Persians from a variety of sources, few of them direct. The Achaemenids left relatively few written records of their own: some monument inscriptions; some tablets inscribed in Elamite, an ancient language of southwestern Iran that is still not very well understood. These sources cannot be compared with the archival treasure houses of the ancient Egyptians or the Hittites, which provide first hand information on national customs, events and personalities. Rather, the scholars lean heavily on what contemporaries had to say about the Persians; they resort to the accounts of Classical Greek historians, official Assyrian and Babylonian chronicles, business documents found in Mesopotamia, private letters written by Egyptians, and the words of Israelite priests and prophets that have come down through the Old Testament. There are also some non-written sources: archaeological evidence deduced from pottery types and building foundations, and from tools and weapons. Sometimes such materials tell the historian more than he can learn from words.

Most important of all, however, are the Greek histories. Despite the techniques of modern archaeology, little more significant information about the Persian Empire is available today than was familiar to any intelligent, concerned citizen of ancient Athens who went to the marketplace to hear read aloud Herodotus' history of the Persian Wars, or chapters from Thucydides, Xenophon and Ctesias—all of whom also wrote extensively about the Persians. Had not the birth of true written history coincided with the rise of the empire, modern scholars would still be at a loss to place this remarkable people in their world context.

Indeed, the relationship of mainland Greece and the Greek colonies of North Africa and Asia Minor to the history of Persia was an intimate one. During the period of Persian ascendancy, the tide of Greek civilization was rising fast. Greek traders were the Persians' most effective mercantile rivals—one fact that led to the war between Persia and the Greek city-states, and resulted in the ultimate defeat of the empire. Arising from that bitter conflict of interests, the bias of the Greek scribes who wrote about Persia is often noticeable, and the modern reader must make allowances for it. But for all that, the corpus of Greek histories written during and after the great flowering of Greek civilization remains at the core of most current understanding of the Persians.

Only in the matter of the Persians' origins has important new material come to light since ancient times. Knowledge of where the Persians came from or how they reached the southwestern corner of the Iranian plateau has been pieced together from the study of ancient languages, from archaeological evidence, and from recently exhumed and translated references found in the records of other kingdoms.

Scholars are thus fairly sure that the Persians were part of a tribal family known as the Iranians, who were members of a still larger group called the Aryans, a scattered assemblage of nomadic tribes whose original homeland was probably the Eurasian plains of southern Russia. Sometime between 2000 and 1800 B.C., the Aryans began to migrate. Some moved to the Indian subcontinent; others turned westwards through Iran and penetrated as far as northern Mesopotamia and Syria. About 1400 B.C., a third group of Aryans—which included the Persians—moved into Iran from the northeast and gradually moved west.

The Iranian plateau they settled on, which Cyrus later praised for the rigorous life it imposed on its inhabitants, is dominated by a ring of rugged mountains, many rising more than 12,000 feet. They surround a central depression of salt deserts that is one of the driest and most unwelcoming regions on the face of the earth. Only in the valleys of the mountain folds or on the plains adjacent to the plateau could substantial numbers of people exist. Extremely hot in summer, sometimes brutally cold in winter, the land was barely suitable for herding.

Journeying west, the Iranian tribes made their way across the plateau, skirting the Elburz Mountains that form its northern edge, and then turned southeast along the Zagros range that separates the plateau from the long-settled, thickly populated, fertile plains of Mesopotamia. In their progress the Iranians shoved out or took over indigenous tribes such as the Guti and Lullubi who had lived in the Zagros for centuries. The newcomers jostled with one another for the choicest territories, stayed for a while, moved on and settled again. The principal tribes of this im-

A Vast and Complex Empire

In less than 70 years, beginning around 560 B.C., Persia's Achaemenid kings brought together all the disparate nations of the ancient Middle East into a single political unit. Within this 2,600-mile-wide expanse (*shaded area*) lay the towering Elburz and Zagros mountains, the fertile valley between the Tigris and Euphrates rivers and the metal-rich hills of Asia Minor.

Achaemenid hegemony reached its peak after 522 B.C. under Darius I. The empire's nucleus had been formed by earlier Achaemenids who, from a base in the region called Persia, laid claim to such ancient kingdoms as Media and Assyria. Cyrus the Great created the actual imperial structure and extended his control to all the land between Bactria and Phrygia. His successor, Cambyses II, absorbed Egypt, and then Darius pushed Persian dominance to its limits. By the end of his reign, the 1,600-mile-long Royal Road connecting the imperial centre at Susa with Sardis in Lydia was completed, as was the canal that joined the Mediterranean with the Red Sea.

The Greek chronicler Herodotus mentioned 28 regions (*large capital letters*) that figured in Persian history; 20 of these were satrapies, or subject states. Scholars have also identified 23 cities and archaeological sites (*small type*) within the Achaemenids' domain.

migrant wave included not only the Persians, but also the Medes—who became their neighbours on the Iranian plateau, and who formed a vital part of their history, first as the Persians' masters, later as their leading vassals.

This historic westward movement was not so much arrested by the physical barrier of the Zagros as by what lay beyond: a civilized world of established states with centuries—in some cases millennia—of cultural, political and military tradition. Northeast of the Zagros Mountains in the lands around Turkey's Lake Van and Iran's Lake Urmia was Urartu, a relatively young but vigorous state. Below Urartu, and on the western edges of the Zagros in modern Iraq, was the empire of the Assyrians. Still farther south was Babylonia, whose capital, Babylon, was the com-

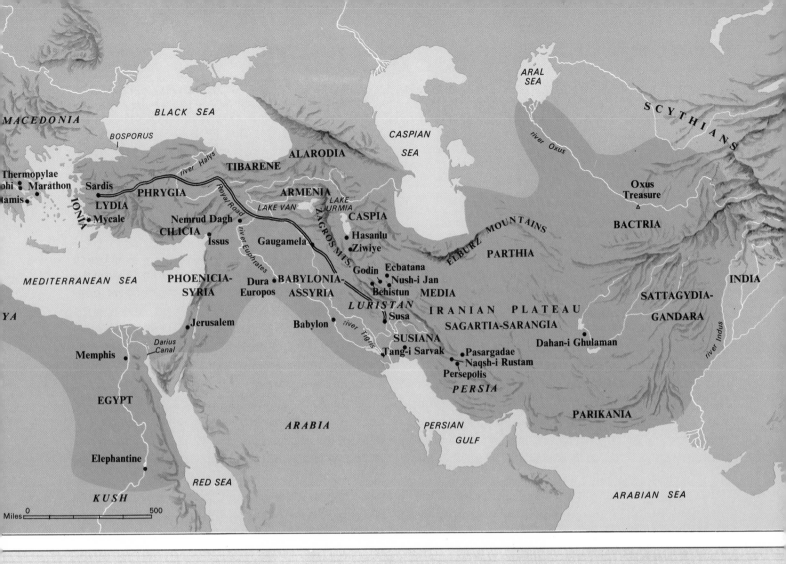

mercial centre of that world. Below Babylonia, at the head of the Persian Gulf, was Elam, with its centre at Susa—a fading, once-brilliant civilization already 2,000 years old.

Looking for lands not controlled by any of these long-established peoples, the Medes finally occupied the wide and fertile plain of present-day Hamadan, in the northwestern corner of the Iranian plateau. The Persians, taking somewhat longer to find a place to their liking, seem to have made several tentative settlements before arriving at the southwestern edge of the plateau and choosing weakly occupied territory in the mountainous back country of Elam. There the Persians ceased their wandering long enough to put down roots and absorb much of the Elamite culture and territory.

Meanwhile, the fountainhead of that culture, ancient Elam, awaited its doom. By the latter half of the Eighth Century B.C., the Assyrians, now the dominant power in the Middle East, had smashed the stubborn resistance of Urartu, brought Babylonia to submission, overcome the small kingdoms of Canaan and conquered Egypt. About 640 B.C. the Assyrian king Ashurbanipal put a violent end to what remained of independent Elam. He boasted that he "transformed the land into a wilderness" and dragged back to Assyria not only the captive people and cattle but the bones of Elam's dead kings. His claims of populations slain, often amounting to genocide, seem not to have been exaggerated.

The former Elamite lands settled by the Persians were apparently too remote and too poor—like the

The horses of the modern Iranian army graze in
pastureland that once nourished the herds
belonging to the imperial Persians' nomadic
ancestors, who migrated from the Eurasian
steppe to the Iranian plateau as early as
2000 B.C. In the background looms the snowy
18,000-foot peak of Mount Demavend, which
is the highest point in the Elburz range.

Persians themselves—to attract the worst furies of
the Assyrian onslaught. But clashes between Assyrians and Medes grew more and more frequent, and
references to "the distant Medes" and "the mighty
Medes of the East" show up in Assyrian annals with
increasing frequency, usually as opponents worthy
of respect. The Assyrians were impressed to find
Medes not only in the Zagros Mountains but as far
east as they could push on to the plateau. Medes
fought from horseback, and from them the Assyrians
learned the use of cavalry. Until then, chariots had
been their only shock force and thereafter many of
their expeditions against the Medes were for the
purpose of acquiring horses.

For their part, the Medes were learning from the
Assyrians the fundamentals of political organization.
To defend themselves the Median tribes united,
forming by about 670 B.C. a state under a single king.
Assyrian power diminished during the late Seventh
Century B.C., partly because unceasing warfare had
sapped their reserves of manpower. With the pressure off, the Medes began building an empire of their
own, and among the peoples on whom they imposed
their sovereignty were the Persians.

The rise of Media is crucial to the history of the Persians, who used the Medes' imperial machinery as
the engine of their own surge to world prominence.

Ecbatana, modern Hamadan, was the Median capital, built athwart the main route from the Fertile
Crescent of the Mesopotamian plains to the Iranian
plateau to central Asia. The Median king, said Herodotus, lived in a palace isolated from his subjects
by seven concentric walls. Only members of the royal
household were permitted to see him and "nobody
was allowed to laugh or spit in the royal presence".
The Greek historian's explanation for these strictures
was perceptive: "If nobody saw him, the legend
would grow that he was a being of a different order
from mere men." It could not have been easy to trans-
form nomadic tribesmen into members of a stable,
cohesive state, and creating an aura of mystery surrounding the supreme leader would have greatly
facilitated the process.

As the Assyrian menace receded, the Medes were
not the only people growing in power. A renascent
Babylonia joined Media in an alliance against Assyria. In this endeavour the Medes apparently did most
of the fighting. A Babylonian chronicle recorded the
fact that the Median king Cyaxares marched on the
Assyrian city of Ashur in 614 B.C., but "the King of
Babylonia and his army . . . did not come in time for
the battle". Even without help, Cyaxares' warriors
"took the town, the wall of the town was torn down,
and they inflicted a terrible massacre upon the entire
population". Two years later the Median and Babylonian armies attacked Nineveh, the Assyrian capital.
After three fierce battles the city was "turned into
ruin-hills and heaps of debris". The Assyrian king
and his military forces escaped, but were finished
off in 609 B.C.

To fuse the link between the victorious parties, a
Median princess married the Babylonian king Nebuchadnezzar—it was for her that he built the famous
Hanging Gardens, supposedly to assuage her home-
sickness for the hills of Media—and the allies began
carving up the spoils. Nebuchadnezzar took the
southern portion of the Assyrian Empire while Cyaxares led his Medes west through Urartu to claim
their share of the booty on the Anatolian plateau.

There the Medes encountered an enemy tougher even than the Assyrians: the Lydians, whose homeland lay in the western portion of Anatolia, along the Aegean coast of modern Turkey. Resisting Cyaxares' invasion, the Lydians fought the conquerors of Assyria to a draw in six difficult campaigns. They were still hard at it when the gods seemingly interceded; during a battle, which astronomers have been able to date precisely to May 28, 585 B.C., "day was suddenly turned into night". Herodotus, who recorded the phenomenon—actually a solar eclipse—noted that its occurrence so unnerved both sides that they promptly made peace.

A stronger influence was probably diplomatic pressure from Babylonia, anxious to have the adversaries settle matters and thus restore opportunities for profitable Anatolian trade, which the long war had interrupted. Media and Lydia accepted the 700-mile-long river Halys as the dividing line between their kingdoms; finally, Cyaxares' son Astyages sealed the treaty by marrying the daughter of the Lydian monarch.

For the next three decades the ancient Middle East experienced a rare period of stability. Nebuchadnezzar grew nervous enough about the ambitions of the Iranians to erect a chain of fortifications, called the Median Wall, along his northern border—stretching from the Tigris to the Euphrates. But basically the power balance among Media, Babylonia and Lydia held fast. In long retrospect it almost appears that this peaceful interlude in the Middle East was a necessary intermission before the main act: the rise of

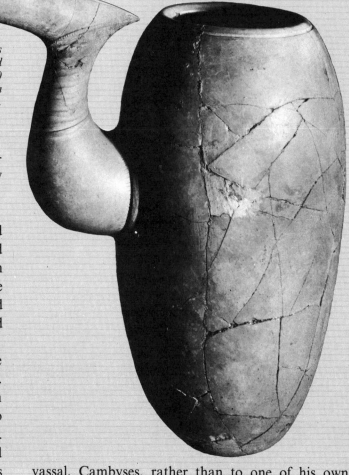

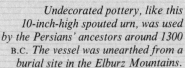

Undecorated pottery, like this 10-inch-high spouted urn, was used by the Persians' ancestors around 1300 B.C. The vessel was unearthed from a burial site in the Elburz Mountains.

Persian power. In developing, that force was to engulf Medes, Lydians, Babylonians—and eventually even the mighty Egyptians.

The region had not long to wait. Sometime around 575 B.C. the wife of a petty Persian king named Cambyses, a Median vassal, gave birth to a son called Kurush, or Cyrus as the Greeks styled the name. He would be Cyrus II, but the world would know him best as Cyrus the Great, architect and founder of the Persian Empire.

Details of the future emperor's genealogy and the circumstances of his birth and childhood are scarce. It is generally accepted that the dynasty into which he was born had been founded by Achaemenes, who ruled the Persians early in the Seventh Century B.C. and gave his name to the succession of Achaemenid kings who followed him. Achaemenes' son Teispes apparently divided the kingdom between his two heirs, Ariaramnes and Cyrus I. The eastern half went to Ariaramnes; the western half, called Anshan, to Cyrus I. Anshan subsequently passed to the elder Cyrus' son Cambyses, father of Cyrus the Great.

When facts are few and the subject is a man of heroic proportions, the human imagination is never reluctant to supply the missing details. The Greek historian Ctesias said that Cyrus II was not of royal birth at all, but the son of a Persian bandit and a shepherdess. Some of the future emperor's countrymen believed that he was reared by a she-wolf that had found him as a baby abandoned in the mountains.

According to the more reliable Herodotus, Cyrus II had Median blood; the historian said that the grandfather was the Median king Astyages, who had married off his daughter Mandane to his Persian

vassal, Cambyses, rather than to one of his own esteemed Medes. His reason for making an inferior marriage for his daughter was a dream Astyages had in which Mandane had expressed deep loathing for him and his kingdom.

In the account by Herodotus, the gods continued to alarm Astyages with similar dreams and so, when Mandane bore Cyrus, the royal grandfather determined to have the infant murdered. He ordered Harpagus, one of his officers, to carry out the deed. But Harpagus could not bring himself to kill the child and hid him with mountain herdsmen, who agreed that they would raise the baby Cyrus to manhood. When Astyages discovered this disobedience, he had Harpagus' own son decapitated and served up the head to the insubordinate father at a banquet. Years later, having waited patiently for revenge, Harpagus went to Cyrus, encouraged him to lead the Persians

Animal figures decorate the spout and sides of this nine-inch-high Iranian jug, set on an openwork stand. Made in the Ninth Century B.C., the pot was found at Hasanlu, in western Iran.

in rebellion and induced the Median army to defect from their king.

Herodotus' account, stripped of romantic embroidery, may well be true. Cyrus II did in fact assume the throne of Anshan in 559 B.C., and then became ruler of all the Persians by subjugating the other branch of the Achaemenids. Soon he began to show signs of independence from his Median overlord, Astyages. The whole process took no more than 10 years.

That Cyrus vaulted to power so rapidly and with so little opposition among the Persians should not be surprising. He was, from all reports, a singularly appealing figure, one of those rare leaders towards whom men cannot help but gravitate. Xenophon, the Greek historian who wrote an admiring biography of Cyrus in the Fourth Century B.C., said that, even in his boyhood, grown men were captivated by Cyrus' wisdom, resilient spirit, guilelessness and physical beauty. The testimony of Nabonidus, King of the Babylonians, indirectly supports Xenophon. The king recorded that the gods themselves were on Cyrus' side, and had come to the sleeping Nabonidus to tell him that Cyrus would soon overthrow the Median ruler Astyages.

By perhaps 550 B.C. the King of the Medes felt compelled to bring his upstart Persian minion into line—but it was indeed too late. Astyages had lost his authority even to command his own army. Nabonidus' Babylonian chronicle went on to tell what happened then: "King Astyages called up his troops and marched against Cyrus, King of Anshan, in order to meet him in battle." The armies met on the high, cheerless plain of Murghab, 400 miles south of the Median capital, near the Persian settlement of Pasargadae. But there was little fighting: "The army of

Astyages revolted against him and in fetters they delivered him to Cyrus."

Along with their king, the Medes surrendered their capital, Ecbatana. Both were treated generously. Astyages' life was spared, and Ecbatana, though denuded of its royal treasures, was otherwise left to prosper. Median officials kept their government posts, although often working alongside Persian opposite numbers. As Cyrus' empire expanded, Medes were second only to Persians in imperial status. To the outside world the Median Empire did not actually fall; it merely underwent a change of management.

The Persians acquired many valuable assets from the Medes: their dominions, their well-organized army—Astyages lost because he was betrayed by his soldiers, not because they lacked fighting skill—and much of their concept of kingship, which emphasized royal rituals and protocol. The Persians also

Prototype for Imperial Palaces

Ruins of a Ninth Century B.C. citadel complex excavated at Hasanlu, near Lake Urmia in northern Iran, have established that the Iranian people who constructed it—possibly a tribe called the Manneans—were master builders. Their pillared halls foreshadow the architectural wonders of Pasargadae and Persepolis—the works of a closely related people: the Persians.

One edifice, whose foundations appear below and in the diagram on the right, may have been a temple. Its central hall, 54 by 72 feet, contained two ceremonial hearths; its roof was once supported by four rows of five columns. Mud-brick benches for notables lined all sides of the hall; one incorporated a platform, perhaps for a throne, with a religious sanctuary behind it.

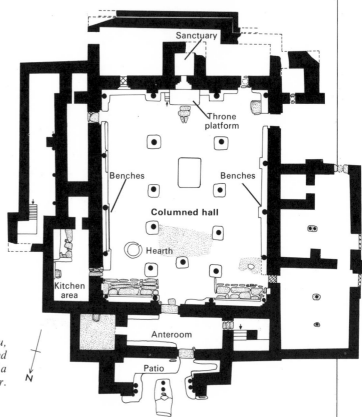

In a ground plan of the temple excavated at Hasanlu, the interior is reached by passing through a portico and an anteroom. Around the main hall are storerooms and a kitchen. Cobbled patches suggest a once-paved floor.

Set among the column bases, two ceremonial hearths—one of them rectangular, the other circular—stand within the main hall.

inherited the old Median rivalry with Lydia, now ruled by a king so rich that his name, Croesus, has ever since been synonymous with extravagant wealth. The Lydian king saw in Astyages' downfall both a challenge to family honour—Astyages was married to Croesus' sister—and an excuse to seize land east of the river Halys that had been denied his father by the Medes. The acquisitive feeling was mutual; Cyrus had his eye on Croesus' vassal states in the western coastal region of Ionia and had already sent agents there to suborn the states' loyalty.

In pursuing his aims, Croesus seems to have been as cautious as he was rich. Herodotus' account of the king's next step bears the stamp of those ancient times, and the historian's reputation for veracity is so formidable that he may be forgiven some touches that can only be the purest fable. Herodotus related that Croesus wanted to consult an oracle about his prospects against Cyrus, but he first set out to determine which of these tellers of the future could be trusted. He sent messengers to more than half a dozen oracular temples—one as far away as Libya—asking the seers to describe what he was doing precisely 100 days after his messengers left his capital of Sardis. The oracle of Delphi won the contest. According to Herodotus, the seer replied that at the time specified the Lydian king was personally boiling a lamb and a tortoise together in a bronze cauldron. In fact, Croesus was doing just that, having deliberately chosen this eccentric enterprise as one that no one would be likely to guess.

Upon hearing his messenger's report, Croesus declared the Delphic oracle "the only genuine one in the world". The messenger was sent to Delphi again, this time bearing valuable gifts. Herodotus described Croesus' offerings to Delphi—which included enormous quantities of ornaments and furnishings decorated in gold and silver—and the historian went on to record where they could still be viewed by travellers in his own day. Along with the Lydian king's gifts, the messenger carried Croesus' real question: Should Lydia go to war with Persia?

The oracle answered that if Croesus crossed the Halys and attacked the Persians, "he would destroy a great empire". The king was so delighted with this cryptic reply that he showered more presents on Delphi—two gold coins for every man in the city. The grateful Delphians responded by granting to Croesus and all Lydians honorary Delphic citizenship, the right to cut in at the head of the line when they wanted to consult the oracle, and front seats at Delphi's state functions.

Meanwhile, Croesus set his war machine in motion. Though he had recently bolstered his position by securing alliances with Egypt, Babylonia and the Greek city of Sparta, he did not even wait for them to send supporting troops. Croesus crossed the Halys in 547 B.C. and captured the former Median fortress of Pteria in the kingdom of Cappadocia. There Croesus awaited Cyrus II, who made the 1,200-mile march to Pteria from the Persian capital at Susa within a few months. The Persian and Lydian armies clashed in early summer outside Pteria. It was a bloody, daylong struggle in which neither the long spears of Lydia's mounted lancers nor the arrows and short swords of the Persian and Median cavalry could sustain an advantage over the opposition. But the Lydians nevertheless left the field. Next morning, claiming he was outnumbered, Croesus headed for Sardis.

Warlike Heritage in Bronze

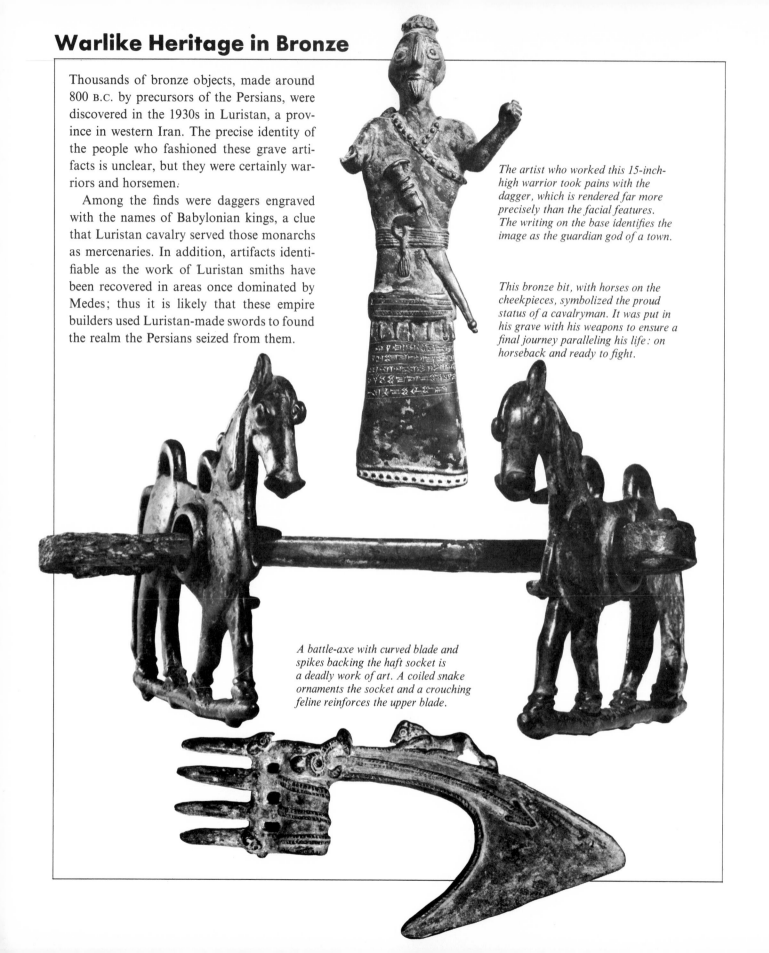

Thousands of bronze objects, made around 800 B.C. by precursors of the Persians, were discovered in the 1930s in Luristan, a province in western Iran. The precise identity of the people who fashioned these grave artifacts is unclear, but they were certainly warriors and horsemen.

Among the finds were daggers engraved with the names of Babylonian kings, a clue that Luristan cavalry served those monarchs as mercenaries. In addition, artifacts identifiable as the work of Luristan smiths have been recovered in areas once dominated by Medes; thus it is likely that these empire builders used Luristan-made swords to found the realm the Persians seized from them.

The artist who worked this 15-inch-high warrior took pains with the dagger, which is rendered far more precisely than the facial features. The writing on the base identifies the image as the guardian god of a town.

This bronze bit, with horses on the cheekpieces, symbolized the proud status of a cavalryman. It was put in his grave with his weapons to ensure a final journey paralleling his life: on horseback and ready to fight.

A battle-axe with curved blade and spikes backing the haft socket is a deadly work of art. A coiled snake ornaments the socket and a crouching feline reinforces the upper blade.

Reaching home he sent messages to his Babylonian, Egyptian and Spartan allies urging them to prepare armies for the next year's operations and began demobilizing his own troops—a normal practice when summer was ending. No one campaigned during the bitter winters of Asia Minor—or so Croesus believed. He had not reckoned on his Persian opponent's strategy of surprise.

Waiting just long enough for the Lydian king to reach Sardis and start paying off his troops, Cyrus advanced so swiftly, Herodotus said, that "he was his own messenger". Croesus hurriedly reassembled his army, putting his redoubtable lancers in the forefront, and went out on the broad plains surrounding his capital to confront the enemy.

But Cyrus had another surprise in store for the Lydians. Knowing that horses instinctively feared camels, he ordered that a large contingent of the humped beasts be brought up from the Persian baggage train, their packs replaced by armed riders, to lead the Persian charge. When the Lydian lancers' horses caught the odour of the unfamiliar animals lumbering towards them, they bolted, shattering the battle order of the entire Lydian force. Despite the mêlée and loss of his cavalry, Croesus and most of his army were able to retreat to safety within the walls of Sardis.

The city, which sat on top of a steep-sided prominence, was widely held to be impregnable; and though Cyrus offered a reward to the first man who could get over the walls, there were no takers for nearly two weeks. It began to seem that only starvation would force the city to yield, and that help from Croesus' allies might arrive before that happened. Then, on the 13th day of the siege, one of Cyrus' warriors observed something interesting. He was camped beneath a side of the fortress that was lightly guarded by the Lydians because its walls were particularly steep. One of the defenders' helmets chanced to fall off and bounce down the incline. Despite the precipitousness of the wall, the helmet's owner was able to scramble down and retrieve his headpiece—and then climb back up. The Persian who watched this feat and carefully marked the route led an attack force up the wall the following day. Sardis was captured and, according to tradition, the humiliated Croesus thereupon had himself burned to death.

After this climactic action, the former subjects of Lydia—notably the Ionian cities on the western coast of Asia Minor, which were populated by Greeks—sent emissaries to the new conqueror offering to renew their vassalage treaties on the same terms they had had with Croesus. Cyrus refused all but one, the city of Miletus. With that powerful potential enemy, the king concluded a separate treaty of friendship and alliance. Meanwhile, he took the other Ionian states on his own terms—forcibly, though he did not personally lead the conquests. He left that duty to subordinates and addressed himself to more urgent business.

First he turned to the east, where he consolidated his hold on the satrapies—or provinces—inherited from the Medes, and added new lands and peoples to his empire. He installed his cousin Hystaspes as governor over the satrapies of Parthia and Hyrcania, to the north and east of the plateau's central desert. In 541 B.C. Cyrus began a march across central Asian plains that are now part of the Soviet Union, subduing one nomadic tribe after another, until he reached the river Jaxartes, today called the Syr Darya. The river, Cyrus declared, was to be his north-eastern frontier; and he built a series of seven fortresses on it to guarantee that the border would not be violated.

Within perhaps a year he had doubled the physical area of his empire and by that achievement had vastly strengthened the size of his army. Cyrus II was now ready to take on his onetime ally, Babylonia. Babylonia was in serious trouble—and hardly ready to repel Cyrus. King Nabonidus, who had come to power as the result of a court conspiracy 17 years earlier, had forfeited the loyalty of his people through religious unorthodoxies, persecutions and general failure to meet his royal responsibilities. Nabonidus was charged with being under the domination of his mother, who was a priestess of the ancient moon god Sin, and with spending freely from the national treasury to construct a temple in the moon god's honour—all the while neglecting Babylonia's chief god, Marduk.

Nabonidus abandoned the capital entirely for an 11-year span during his reign while he went off on a military expedition designed to control the caravan routes and trade along the Persian Gulf. Year after year his heretical behaviour was noted in the history of the times: "The king did not come to Babylon for the ceremony of the month of Nisanu [March-April] .... The god Marduk did not go out in procession.... The festival of the New Year was omitted."

The absentee king entrusted the running of Babylonia and the control of its home army to his son Prince Belshazzar who, according to the Bible, was foretold of his doom by the "writing on the wall". "You are found wanting," he was warned. "Your

Bastion of the Formidable Medes

Until the giant fortress-manor at Godin, located near the ancient Median capital of Ecbatana, was excavated beginning in 1965, no first-hand information about the Medes existed. Those fierce and canny warriors were known chiefly through the historic accounts provided by other ancient peoples, probably the Assyrians, the Jews and the Greeks.

Perched at the top of a mound above a sheer drop of 80 feet, the sprawling structure at Godin—with its thick walls, battlemented turrets and rows of magazines for the storage of weapons and provisions—resembles a medieval stronghold. Three rectangular, columned halls, similar in design and concept to those at Hasanlu and Pasargadae, point to the cultural bond between the Medes and other Iranians—particularly their eventual rulers, the Persians. The fortress proved as impregnable as it looks; it was never captured, only abandoned voluntarily by its occupants, possibly in a move to concentrate Median power at Ecbatana.

In this relief from the palace at Dur Sharrukin in Iraq, soldiers of the Assyrian monarch Sargon II attack a Median fortress similar to the one excavated at Godin. Powerful Assyria repeatedly attempted to crush the Medes but failed.

The 350-foot-long northern wall of the Median fortress, with its buttresses and recesses, still commands the precipitous heights at Godin.

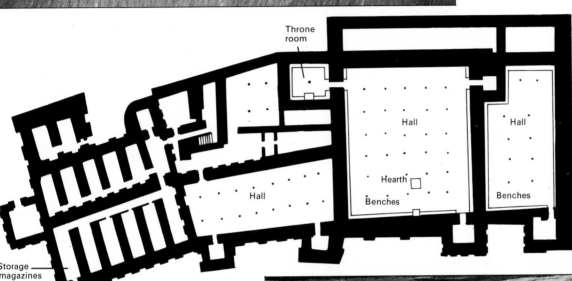

The ground plan of the fortress includes two sets of storage magazines, each comprising 11 compartments; three pillared halls, the largest of which contained 30 freestanding columns (dots); a small square throne room to the right of what might have been an anteroom; and along the lower edge of the plan five towers that at one time were manned for defence.

This staircase led to an upper storey, no longer in existence, which probably contained the living quarters of the fortress. A corridor to the right of the stairs led to the southern magazine bins (upper left in the plan above).

In a drawing based on a Greek vase painting, Croesus of Lydia—one of many kings defeated by Persia's Cyrus the Great—awaits a fiery death; from his pyre he makes a last ritual wine offering as a servant kindles the blaze. This version of Croesus' death is based on an account that held that the mortified Lydian attempted suicide. But the historian Herodotus wrote that Cyrus condemned Croesus to death by fire.

kingdom is finished." The words confirmed what had long been obvious: the inevitability of Cyrus' attack.

Still swayed by his own religious obsession, but now mindful of the danger, Nabonidus returned to Babylon and began bringing into his capital, for safekeeping, images of the gods from other cities of the empire. The moves were in one sense prudent, but they only angered his subjects more. Marduk, they knew, would not look kindly on Babylon playing host within his own city to all these competing gods; and at the same time the transplanted gods were no longer protecting the cities that had relied upon them for generations.

In 540 B.C., his 19th year as King of the Persians, Cyrus launched his campaign against Babylon. He probably spent the whole summer getting his army across the river Gyndes, an unfordable tributary of the Tigris. To do so, he launched an ingenious engineering project. Not one to be daunted by the greater strength of an adversary, human or natural, Cyrus had his troops conquer the river with shovels; they redirected its course into many separate, shallow channels. Then Cyrus' armies crossed to the south bank of the river, entered Babylonia behind the Median Wall, its main defence line, and dispatched the Babylonian army in a battle near the city of Opis.

Two days later—only 16 days after the combat at Opis—Gobryas, a Babylonian governor who had gone over to Cyrus' service, led his own troops and part of the Persian army into Babylon "without battle". They guarded Marduk's temple, made sure that all the traditional ceremonies were observed, and saw that the city's busy commercial life continued uninterrupted. The only excitement seems to have been the arrival of Nabonidus, who rushed into his

capital seeking refuge, only to find it occupied and himself a captive.

Cyrus, by contrast, arrived shortly afterwards to a generous welcome. "Green twigs were spread in front of him," recorded a chronicler, and peace was imposed upon the city. "To the inhabitants of Babylon a joyful heart is given now," concluded the chronicler. "They are like prisoners when the prisons are opened."

If the people did have any fears about the new regime, Cyrus quickly reassured them. He sent greetings to all of Babylon and presented himself not as a foreign conqueror but as King of Babylon, personally selected by Marduk, who, in the words of a chronicle commissioned by Cyrus, had "scanned and looked through all the countries searching for a righteous ruler". Cyrus himself worshipped Marduk daily; and he returned the gods that Nabonidus had commandeered to their legitimate abodes throughout the kingdom. Furthermore, he kept his army under tight control. As he stated in a proclamation to the Babylonians, "My numerous troops walked around in Babylon in peace. I did not allow anybody to terrorize the country." Tactfully, he allowed most of the officers of the government to remain at their posts, showing once again his remarkable capacity to trust his former enemies and thereby gain their loyalty.

In winning Babylonia, the Persians acquired more than the world's greatest commercial city and the immensely productive agricultural lands of Mesopotamia. Soon Cyrus could exultantly proclaim that kings from Babylonia's dominions "brought their heavy tribute and kissed my feet". Among those dominions was Phoenicia, whose fleet would prove the greatest prize of all; with the ships and seamen of Phoenicia at their disposal, the Persians became a great sea power—only 10 years after venturing from their small inland kingdom.

This consolidation of Persian might fired Cyrus' ambitions anew, and he began preparations for fresh conquests. Within a year he freed Babylonia's Israelites, who had been held captive there since 589 B.C., gave them back the silver and gold treasures looted from their temple in Jerusalem, and sent them home, 40,000 strong. The magnanimous gesture was perfectly in line with his policy of justice and religious freedom for his subjects. But it also secured for him the gratitude and loyalty of a Canaanite people, and Canaan controlled the land route—just as his new Phoenician fleet controlled the sea route—to the last great country still outside the Persian Empire: old, storied, wealthy Egypt.

But Cyrus never reached Egypt. With the conquest of Babylonia, the area, population, wealth and power of the Persian Empire had swollen to gigantic proportions. Cyrus must have been occupied for some time in adjusting his own governmental apparatus to regulate the immense territories under his sway. There were satrapies to organize; satraps, or governors, to appoint; new vassals to receive; tributes to accept; armies to absorb into the great Persian war machine; and justice to dispense. Cyrus was also busy embellishing his imperial residence, which was slowly rising at Pasargadae, scene of his crucial victory over the Medes.

When at last he might have had time to sit down to plan an Egyptian campaign, news of trouble came from the east. Nomads ruled by Queen Tomyris were threatening his frontier provinces. Cyrus ordered countermeasures, and led the expedition himself.

Characteristically, he pursued the enemy into their own territory where, in 530 B.C., the fierce tribesmen united and gave battle, said by Herodotus to be "more violent than any other fought". Most of the Persians were killed, including Cyrus. His body was carried home to Pasargadae and placed in the royal tomb that Cyrus had designed for himself.

Inevitably, the affairs of Cyrus' huge realm turned chaotic upon his death. His son Cambyses II inherited the throne and successfully pursued his father's plans for the conquest of Egypt. But then Cambyses himself died, and the ensuing years were a time of conflicting claims to the Persian throne that nearly brought the great empire crashing down.

Along with the kingship, Cambyses II had inherited some of his father's administrative and military talents, as well as his designs on Egypt. But he did not, apparently, inherit Cyrus' popularity. Cyrus had long before named Cambyses King of Babylon, retaining for himself the greater title of King of the Lands. Cambyses had resided in and ruled that huge province for eight years, adhering to Cyrus' policy of keeping high Babylonian dignitaries in their offices. But unlike his father, he had in his dealings with

Persian and foreign subjects alike acquired notoriety as a despot.

Cambyses was said to have killed one of his wives —who was also his sister—by kicking her when she was pregnant, and to have shot the son of one of his closest attendants with an arrow, just to demonstrate his skill at archery. Herodotus reported that Cambyses had 12 high-ranking Persians buried alive "on some trifling charge". The king allegedly drank heavily and when in his cups continually asked people what they thought of him, which in light of his reputation for rage and the Persians' ingrained respect for truth must have generated some very quick thinking around the imperial court. One of Cambyses' advisors apparently found a near-ideal reply. Herodotus quoted him this way: "I do not think you are equal to your father; for you have not yet a son like the son he left behind him in yourself." In considering Cambyses, the historian concluded that the Persian king was "completely out of his mind".

But Cambyses' achievement in following through his father's plans for Egypt indicates otherwise. In a swift campaign of about a year's duration, Cambyses defeated the Egyptian army and, by May of 525 B.C., was installed on the throne of the pharaohs. As soon as that news circulated, Libya and the Greek cities of Barca and Cyrene on the North African coast obligingly sent their surrenders by messenger. Added to Ionia and to the big Greek colonies in Egypt itself, these acquisitions meant that Persia, at this early date, already ruled half the Greek world. But Cambyses wanted more. Driven perhaps by a need to surpass his father, he wished to create an African empire as great as his Asian one.

Here Cambyses' luck ran out. When he was set to move against Carthage, his Phoenician sailors, whose ships were indispensable to the project, refused to attack their Carthaginian kinsmen. To conquer an inland colony of Greeks at the Siwa Oasis, in the Egyptian desert, he sent—Herodotus said—a full army of 50,000 men. But all the expedition's members died or deserted en route. Cambyses personally led a large force against the kingdom of Kush, which included the Sudan. After penetrating farther south into Africa than had any previous Asian conqueror —two-thirds the distance to the Kushite capital of Meröe—he had to turn back, possibly because of poor logistical preparations for the long march. Except for the establishment of a garrison at Elephantine, an island in the Nile near Aswan, nothing further came of Cambyses' plans for an African empire.

In 522 B.C., after three years in Egypt, Cambyses was called back to Persia in order to deal with a political crisis—a usurper was sitting on his throne. Cambyses died on his way home and Darius, one of his officers in Egypt and a distant cousin, succeeded him after dislodging the pretender. But the precise circumstances of Darius' accession are even today the subject of some scholarly controversy.

The official version—disseminated by Darius nearly 2,500 years ago and still widely accepted—asserted that Cambyses' brother, named Smerdis, was secretly executed on the king's orders before going to Egypt. The murder was done to prevent Smerdis from taking the throne in Cambyses' absence. While the king was gone, Gaumata, one of the hereditary priests of the Magi tribe, seized the opportunity to impersonate Smerdis. It was upon learning of this treachery that Cambyses started back to oust Gau-

mata. Darius, according to his own explanation, simply fulfilled the king's intent by disposing of the usurper. But he then had to put down rebellions all over the empire, some led by other pretenders who had been inspired by Gaumata's example.

A modern interpretation of the events—one that has evolved as knowledge of Achaemenid history and mores has increased—assumes that the real Smerdis was alive when Cambyses went to Egypt. In the king's absence, Smerdis—being ambitious and enjoying a popularity that Cambyses had never known—seized the throne with the general approval of his subjects. But Darius and other Persian nobles took advantage of the time of confusion after Cambyses' death to dispose of Smerdis, and Darius was made king. It was this plot that led to the open rebellions Darius put down; only later did he concoct the story about the imposter Gaumata to legitimatize his own claim to the throne.

Whichever view of these events contains the core of truth, Darius went to considerable efforts to broadcast his version of how he came to power, ordering a royal autobiography to be circulated to all corners of the empire. He also had the official account inscribed in three languages—Old Persian, Elamite and Akkadian—on a rock face more than 300 feet above the main caravan route from Ecbatana to Babylon, near the village of Behistun. The cliff was a curious site on which to make political statements; the inscriptions could not possibly be read by anyone on the ground, and once the carvers had finished, the rock face itself could not be approached even by the most intrepid climbers; the cliff below was chiselled smooth, precisely in order to prevent vandals from getting up to the inscriptions. The

Behistun reliefs seem, rather, to have been intended for the gods and posterity.

In the inscriptions Darius described the moment of his intervention as a time of great distress. "The people feared Gaumata the pretender greatly," Darius said, "thinking that he would slay the people who previously had known Smerdis. . . . No one dared say anything about Gaumata the Magian until I came. Then I with a few men slew Gaumata the Magian, and those who were his foremost followers." Darius then went on to tell of the rebellions and of how his army fought 19 battles and defeated nine would-be kings, all within "one and the same year".

Darius' explanation of the affair was not seriously challenged by historians until the 1930s when the late A. T. Olmstead of the University of Chicago's Oriental Institute took up the issue. In questioning Darius' version, Olmstead and other sceptics have asked some basic questions: Why would Cambyses, who had no sons, murder his only heir and foreclose his line's possession of the throne? How could the king's brother be dead for three years without anyone's noticing the absence? If "the people universally were pleased" by Darius' actions, why did rebellions break out, even in Persia itself? Finally, does Darius not prove himself a liar by claiming to have put down all those revolts within a single year?

Reinforcing these doubts—and others—is the fact that Darius seems to have anticipated objections and tried to discount them in advance. In the Behistun text he repeatedly urged the reader to believe his story. "Let that which has been done by me convince you; do not think it a lie." Again: "This is true, not false." And finally Darius claimed he really did much more that was not in the record, and insisted the full

Text continued on page 33

Symbols of Might for the King of Kings

Young Darius was only 29 when this first royal portrait was carved at Behistun. The full stiff beard, the thicket of ringlets at the nape of the neck and the flat curls pressed to the forehead are stylistic elements based on renderings of Assyrian sovereigns whose reigns preceded Darius.

When Darius the Great ascended the Achaemenid throne in 522 B.C., the Persian Empire was newly forged. The royal office still lacked the mechanisms and emblems of sovereignty used by older monarchies such as Egypt, Assyria and Babylonia. So the king made it his first order of business to endow the throne with an effective managerial structure and appropriate symbols of supreme power.

To that end, he pragmatically adapted the practices he observed in other realms; introducing few new concepts, he developed and aggrandized other people's ideas brilliantly. For example, the complex system of justice by which Darius ruled had a simpler prototype in ancient Mesopotamian law. The coinage he used to unify the entire commercial world of his time was a Lydian invention. Similarly, the protocol and ceremony with which he surrounded his own office was based on the court rituals of his neighbours and conquered territories.

Thus, it is not surprising that the portraits Darius ordered of himself followed the style of works commissioned by other rulers. As befitted the King of Kings, however, his images were prouder and more monumental than those of foreign counterparts. But significantly, while he never allowed his subjects to see him as less than all-powerful, in representations that show the monarch and his god together, the deity takes precedence.

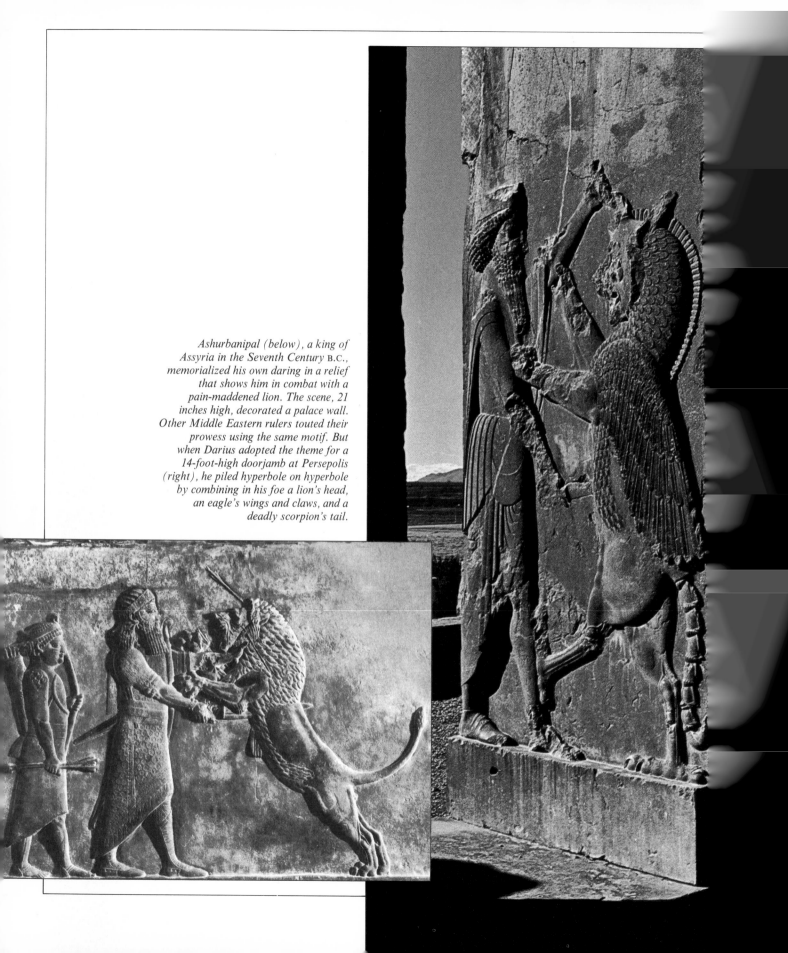

Ashurbanipal (below), a king of Assyria in the Seventh Century B.C., *memorialized his own daring in a relief that shows him in combat with a pain-maddened lion. The scene, 21 inches high, decorated a palace wall. Other Middle Eastern rulers touted their prowess using the same motif. But when Darius adopted the theme for a 14-foot-high doorjamb at Persepolis (right), he piled hyperbole on hyperbole by combining in his foe a lion's head, an eagle's wings and claws, and a deadly scorpion's tail.*

To commemorate Darius' rise to power, this 40-foot-long relief at Behistun (above) was carved in 521 B.C., the second year of his reign. While captured rebel leaders stand by, the king's foot rests on the body of Gaumata, the pretender he overthrew. The composition was obviously inspired by a five-foot-wide, 21st Century B.C. Iranian rock carving (drawing), found at Sar-i Pul near Behistun, in which a chieftain stands in a similar pose with a beaten enemy.

In a throne hall relief at Persepolis, Darius sits on a throne borne by figures symbolizing 28 subject peoples. Significantly, the king placed the winged image of his deity, Ahuramazda, above his own head. But the treatment suggests that reliefs like the one below, of the 12th Century B.C. pharaoh Ramses III, caught Darius' eye when he campaigned in Egypt and were prototypes for his own monument. However, the pharaoh, believing himself divine, is carried by his princes and had himself portrayed as a god.

listing of his accomplishments would have strained the reader's credulity, and thus cast doubt on his motives—and on the legitimacy of his claim.

For all the weaknesses in Darius' case, he has his defenders. Historians who accept his version have offered plausible, if equally speculative, answers to rebut the sceptics. For instance, the statement that Darius overwhelmed the rebels and pretenders within a year is explained by adjusting for certain very real eccentricities in the way contemporary scribes recorded dates. Through such extrapolations, Darius' claim that he accomplished so much in "one year" can be interpreted as referring to a span actually closer to two years. The rebellions could reasonably have been put down in that much time.

Whether or not the reader of the Behistun inscriptions believes their insistent royal author, all the scholarly authorities agree that in 522 and 521 B.C. violent conflicts shook the Persian homeland and threatened to topple the empire. Persia's conquered provinces exploited the uncertain conditions to reassert their own sovereignties. Very shortly after Darius took over, a man calling himself Nebuchadnezzar III, the son of Nabonidus, was acknowledged in Babylon as king. Almost simultaneously in Susa, a new king of Elam declared his accession.

Within three months Darius had executed both of these rebels. But while he was personally commanding the campaign in Babylonia, new insurrections broke out in Persia, Elam, Media, Assyria, Parthia, Margiana, Sattagydia and among the nomads on the eastern frontier. Darius never faltered. He moved rapidly from province to province and back again, dispatched armies to relieve his beleaguered but loyal satraps, and cannily sent Medes to subdue rebelling Persians, and Persians to attack Medes.

Darius was unforgiving of the rebels; he had the leaders publicly flayed and impaled. By the end of 521 B.C.—after the defeat of yet another Babylonian king named Nebuchadnezzar and a third upstart Elamite king in Susa—Darius had quelled the rebellions. The empire was still in one piece.

Darius was now recognized as king over troubled lands comprising nearly a million and a half square miles. Whether his credentials were valid or his claim just, he was the man to match the task at hand and he knew it, though he couched his assertion of self-confidence in properly religious terms: "Ahuramazda, when he saw this earth in commotion, bestowed it upon me, made me king."

Fortunately for him and the empire, Darius' appeal as a leader was in a class with that of Cyrus. On Cambyses' Egyptian campaign Darius had been commander of the army's elite corps, the Ten Thousand Immortals—so called because when men died or were disabled, they were immediately replaced; in this way, the corps' strength never fell below 10,000. These troops followed Darius faithfully throughout the period of the rebellions. Compared with most ancient kings, inveterate braggarts who vaunted their superhuman powers and glorious deeds across the fronts of public buildings and on statues of themselves, Darius was actually a relatively modest man. The qualities in which he took pride were simple and forthright: "I am a friend to right, I am not a friend to wrong. I am not hot-tempered. What things develop in my anger, I hold firmly under control by my thinking power. I am a good fighter."

The straightforwardness of Darius' character was clearly reflected in the steps he took after the internecine fighting stopped. While he consolidated order and saw to the administration of his huge realm, the new ruler allowed his defeated foes a three-year moratorium on military service obligations and three years' remission of taxes. To be sure, he balanced such conciliatory measures with a convincing appearance of firmness; at the least sign of weakness, the provincial governors would surely have tried once again to gain independence. Then, when conditions permitted, Darius made plans to extend the empire.

In this endeavour, Darius proved to be Cyrus' spiritual descendant. Unlike Cyrus, however, Darius seems to have been more concerned with political and economic objectives than military goals, though a few details of the campaign have come down in Greek histories that are corroborated by Darius' inscription at Behistun. Sometime during the seven years after 521 B.C. he led his armies back to the gates of India, where a quarter century earlier Cyrus had been content to fix the eastern limits of his empire. Darius wanted the whole of western India as far as the river Indus—and he took it. The new province, Hindush, where gold dust ran in the streams, became the richest source of revenue in the empire.

Darius' next great campaign also embraced long-range economic motives: the undermining of mainland Greece as a trade rival in the Mediterranean. As was Darius' style, he went about it on a colossal scale, calling up hundreds of engineers, shipbuilders and a huge army. Herodotus offered the astonishing total of 700,000 men in Darius' land forces, though modern historians tend to discount that figure; one estimate places the army's number at closer to 70,000. In 513 B.C. work was finished on a floating bridge linking the two shores of the Bosporus Strait near modern Istanbul. Darius gave the order to advance and the first organized military invasion of Europe by Asians was underway.

The immediate objective of the massive expedition, which included 300 to 600 ships in addition to the infantry and mounted troops, was to subdue the warlike Getai of Thrace and the Scythian nomads who lived between the Danube and the Don rivers. In so doing, Darius hoped to cut off the traffic in supplies of grain and shipbuilding timber that originated in the Balkan hinterland and were essential to the prosperity of European Greece.

Darius marched through Thrace with little resistance. His Scythian offensive, on the other hand, proved a failure. Reaching a suitable place on the Danube, the imperial army crossed on another bridge of boats and meandered aimlessly over the steppes for two months, never able to bring the Scythians to a decisive battle. Neither could they find food; the Scythians burned their own fields and storehouses as they retreated. Herodotus said that the Persians became so desperate that they abandoned their sick and wounded before heading back to the Danube bridge. They arrived just in time; their Ionian allies, having given up hope for the expedition, were about to withdraw their ships.

Darius returned home, but left behind an army that completed the conquest of Thrace and Macedonia. Already King of Kings, lord of Asia and master of Africa, he was now a major force in Europe. Darius had achieved his dream—rescuing the empire from disintegration and raising it to domination of the civilized world. But his true genius, unmatched in his time, lay in his capacity for running the huge, unwieldy imperial machine he had built.

Tribute from a Parade of Nations

"I am Xerxes, the Great King . . . King of countries containing all kinds of men, King in this great earth far and wide." This sweeping assertion—which the Persian ruler ordered inscribed on the two staircases of his monumental apadana, or audience hall, at Persepolis—was no empty boast. The statement is attested to by carvings on the stone façades of the stairways, which show processions of representatives coming to pay the king homage from the more than 30 Persian satrapies and client nations that sprawled across most of the known world in Xerxes' time.

Sometimes—as in the reliefs that appear on these pages, recording the spring New Year's festival—the emissaries arrived bearing gifts of fabric and wares, which they laid at their sovereign's feet. There are no clues to the actual types of cloth and metal used. But scholars are proceeding to establish the nationalities of the unidentified figures by examining carvings on Persian royal tombs inscribed with legends that label regional origins. Meanwhile, these parading delegates provide a pageant in stone of ancient dress, crafts and goods.

A Mede carrying a pitcher is part of the delegation that heads the staircase procession at Persepolis. Because Medes were the king's most favoured subjects, they had the honour of leading the train of gift bearers.

Captive Peoples at the Empire's Core

A delegate from the region of Elam, located in southwestern Iran, clutches a lion cub, an appropriate gift for the mightiest monarch of the ancient world. Like the Babylonians and Assyrians (right), the Elamites were a central nation of the Persian Empire and once-powerful people who could look back on conquests of their own.

Representatives of Babylonia—one of the most fertile satrapies and noted for its livestock—include among their presents a prize bull, lengths of fabric (possibly wool) and banquet bowls. As a sign of friendly dominance, the Persian usher assigned to guide the emissaries to the audience hall grasps the Babylonian leader's hand.

On behalf of their formerly mighty nation, now conquered and impoverished, Assyrians offer such simple presents as dressed animal skins and a pair of rams chosen from their flocks. Once feared throughout the Middle East, the bellicose Assyrians had ruled an empire stretching from the Persian Gulf to the Nile Valley.

Wealthy Merchants from Anatolia

Ionians, whose thriving merchant centres on the west coast of Asia Minor produced fine metalwork and fabric, pledge allegiance with what appear to be beehives, bolts of cloth that may be linen, and dishes—probably of gold. The cities of Ionia, founded by Greek colonists about 1000 B.C., were subdued by the neighbouring Lydians (right) and came under Persian rule just after Cyrus the Great defeated the Lydians.

The distinctive locks of hair dangling behind the ears mark these men as Lydians. Among the most affluent of the Persians' subject peoples, the Lydians owed their wealth to trade and to the yield of their local gold mines. The vessels being presented to the king were very likely fashioned of Lydian gold. The graceful vases, with animal figures adorning each handle, were especially favoured by the Achaemenids.

Hardy Stockbreeders
of the North

A Bactrian camel dominates a frieze devoted to subjects from the country east of the Caspian Sea. Scholars are unsure whether the figures are Bactrians—a supposition borne out by the camel—or their neighbours, the Parthians, who were chiefly horse breeders, but whose dress was marked by the wrinkled trousers that the men in this relief are wearing.

In this portrayal of two Scythians—skilled horsemen and smiths—one carries metal armlets and a sword. Bearing a weapon in the royal presence was a privilege given to few vassals, suggesting that these nomads from north of the Black Sea were probably Persian allies rather than subjects.

This superb stallion was a royal gift from the Armenians, people from the cold upland region west of the Caspian Sea who were envied for their spirited horses—some bred especially for their Persian overlords. The vase, whose handles are ornamented with winged griffins, is an example of the elegant metalwork for which the Armenians were famous.

Africans and Indians with Opulent Gifts

An African tribute bearer carries
an elephant tusk and leads an
okapi—exotic presents from the
southernmost regions of the empire.
He was probably a Kushite, from what
is now the Sudan. Some Kushites
came under Persian domination
with the conquest of Egypt.

Gold dust from the Indus Valley, the
eastern limit of Achaemenid power,
probably filled the containers borne on a
yoke by the Indian on the far right. Traces
of the gold such subjects washed from
their rivers are still found in the
Ganges and in some tributaries of
the Indus—particularly the Sutlej.

The administrative apparatus constructed by the early kings of Persia, particularly by Darius, was a marvel of workability. So solid, in fact, were the overall accomplishments of the Persians in operating their enormous political enterprise that their record can be read almost like a textbook on empire building, offering solutions—devised by experts—to most of the problems of imperial statecraft.

The empire derived its fundamental energy from the authority of the king himself. Though threatened from time to time by potentially rebellious subjects, haphazard succession procedures or intrigues among the members of the court, this sovereignty was carefully maintained under the divine sponsorship of the supreme god Ahuramazda and buttressed by an immutable body of law based on precedent and—ultimately—on the undisputed word of the king.

This royal authority was exerted through a sophisticated governmental system: a bureaucracy headed by Persian nobles; a corps of scribes to keep records; a treasury to collect revenues and make disbursements, particularly for state-sponsored building programmes; and a smooth-running communications network. Finally, the Persians gathered the fruits of empire from the far-flung satrapies and colonies that they had conquered with the help of a mobile, well-trained military and naval organization.

Among the most notable attributes of this managerial structure was the Achaemenids' ability to organize it relatively early in their history. When the Persians came to power in the middle of the Sixth Century B.C., they began with an immense advantage; they did not have to take time to invent the basic framework of their imperial administration, or even to bother with creating many of its external trappings. They inherited these institutions, in more or less rudimentary form, from various other Middle Eastern empires (*pages 29-32*); and many of the fundamental concepts came to the Persians from their kinsmen and former overlords, the Medes. Whatever the source, however, the older modes proved remarkably adaptable to the Persians' own requirements, though the Achaemenid system was larger in scale.

To be sure, this process of assimilation and implementation took place in stages; it was not until the reign of Darius that the imperial mechanism began to gather real momentum. Cyrus, for example, did little to develop the particular administrative institutions that would later sustain the new empire and for which it would be remembered. His single step in this direction was the creation of a royal office to rule over the combined Persian tribes; in general his concept of kingship was modest compared with the kind of supremacy that Darius and his successors would insist upon.

Indeed, the whole idea of kingship was fairly new to the Persians; Cyrus' generation was only about 100 years removed from the time of its tribal forebears, among whom royalty did not exist. Organized in 10 or more tribes, these early Persians probably elected their leaders, at least to the extent of following them by acclamation. In later generations it became customary among the nomadic Persians

This gold drinking cup probably graced a Persian king's table in the Fifth Century B.C. The leonine monster that forms the handle represents a protector-spirit for both the vessel's contents and the royal user. But to assure the monarch's safety from poison, a courtier tasted the drink—most likely wine—before the sovereign put the cup to his lips.

for the sons and grandsons of popular headmen to succeed their kinsmen, giving rise to a dominant clan within each tribe—though the right of the tribe to reject such heirs was nominally intact. By the time of Cyrus the principle of a ruling class was strongly entrenched, but it took a man of Cyrus' energy and charisma to win a number of other tribal leaders to his standard and persuade them to unite behind him. Cyrus won this solidarity by diplomacy; he dominated his princes not as an absolute ruler but as "first among equals", the chief of a royal council that governed a confederation of tribes. Later, when the Persian Empire was a reality, Cyrus held it together with policies of fairness and tact that complemented his military strength.

Cyrus' son Cambyses, undistinguished for his ability to lead men, almost permitted the newly founded empire to slip away during the brief eight years of his reign; and it was precisely because no overwhelming right of kingship was yet attached to the Achaemenid name that other claimants were quick to appear and collect rival followings. Darius, as his second cousin, probably had the strongest legal claim to the throne, but nonetheless he had to unseat a successful pretender before he could restore the monarchy to the Achaemenid family.

Even then the succession was not stabilized. Near the end of Darius' 36-year reign, the problem arose again. As Herodotus described the situation, the issue was prompted by Darius' preparations for a military expedition. By custom, the king was expected to announce his heir before going into battle, in case he should lose his life. But the law of succession was unwritten and ambiguous. Darius had married before his accession and again after he became king, siring sons by each wife. The first-born of each marriage—Artabazanes, who was older, and the younger Xerxes—heatedly argued their separate claims before the king. Then, while Darius was still considering his decision, the exiled king of Sparta arrived in the Persian capital. Seeing an opportunity to win a useful ally by intervening in the squabble, the Spartan visited Xerxes and gave him some advice.

He urged the younger man to remind his father that since Darius already ruled Persia at Xerxes' birth, Xerxes had been born a royal prince, and was therefore a natural heir to the throne—unlike Artabazanes, who had been born before his father held any public office. Xerxes was delighted with the Spartan's suggestion and went back to make his case with his father once more.

Darius, seeing the logic in appointing a son born under the special protection of the crown, thereupon proclaimed Xerxes his heir. For the moment, the crisis had been resolved; but the fact that such crucial matters of state could be influenced by this sort of invention would prove to be an eternally vexing weakness in the system.

In every other department, however, Darius strengthened his regime. He made his office the highest authority throughout the empire and his royal personage the symbol of imperial unity. The image was reinforced by the splendour and comfort in which the king and his retinue lived.

To begin with, the royal household included many personal attendants, often highborn men. While most came of Persian or Median families, some foreigners found a place in royal favour. (Nehemiah, the Jew described in the Old Testament book of that name, was for a time cupbearer to Xerxes' successor, King Artaxerxes; in that role Nehemiah was specifically entrusted with ensuring that everything the king drank had been sampled by a tester and was free of poison; in practice the cupbearer also functioned as a kind of private secretary.)

The king's perquisites included a royal harem. It was a sizeable community, including the king's wives —Darius had four, and other monarchs may have had many more—and his concubines, selected from the most attractive women in the realm. Also living within the walls might be the queen mother, the king's unmarried sisters, a throng of royal offspring including the crown prince, and a contingent of eunuchs. By the custom of the ancient world, these harem servants came from among Persia's subject peoples, and were emasculated before being placed in positions of personal responsibility to the royal family. In later years the harem was to increase dangerously in political influence, becoming a hothouse of sprouting plots and blossoming intrigues. But in Darius' era, it was not yet a source of trouble.

A high degree of ceremony was intrinsic in the maintenance of royal authority. Even in the conduct of day-to-day business, protocol was always smartly observed. The Biblical Book of Esther, which provides interesting details of Persian court life, says that subjects entered the ruler's presence only upon explicit invitation. For anyone so foolish as to transgress against this regulation, "there is one law only: that person shall be put to death"—unless the king signalled with a wave of his golden sceptre that the subject's life be spared. Actually, certain high nobles at court were exempted from this harsh rule, but they were expected to bow low and to kiss their own hands upon approaching the king. Commoners, allowed only in rare instances to come before him, began by throwing themselves face down on the ground before the throne, where they waited until the sovereign bade them stand.

An important aspect of this protocol rested on an assumption about the source of royal power, which was held to be divine. Persian monarchs presumably adapted this concept from earlier Mesopotamian kings, who believed that their reigns were sanctioned by patron gods. Achaemenid rulers from Darius' time on claimed a similar divine right, asserting that they were the chosen agents of Ahuramazda, the supreme god of the Persians. Characteristically, the early Achaemenids made canny political use of the claimed right when dealing with conquered peoples; they attributed divine sanction of their rule to the authority of Marduk, or the Egyptian god Ra, or whatever local divinity might be worshipped by a vanquished populace, and honoured that god accordingly.

This assumed delegation of power from deity to king was the moral crux of the absolute royal prerogative to make and adjudicate the law. However, the ruler was bound by tradition to consult with his high officers and other nobles before arriving at crucial decisions. For example, court judges, called law bearers, were supposed to advise the monarch on customary law as it applied to a particular situation, but their decisions were not always binding. The judges were unwilling to bend the law but equally disinclined to hand down a decision displeasing to the king. In certain rare instances, when pressed for a justification that could not strictly conform to the law, they delivered an ambiguous verdict and left the sovereign to interpret it.

How this advisory system worked in practice can be seen in a story Herodotus related about Cambyses. Wishing to marry his sister, Cambyses asked the law bearers whether such a match was permissible. The judges believed it was wrong, but were reluctant to risk Cambyses' notorious wrath by giving him an answer they knew he did not want to hear. So they replied that while they could not find a law allowing him to marry his sister, they thought there surely was another law that said a Persian king was entitled to do whatever he pleased. The emperor and everyone else were well satisfied.

Though the law could be made flexible when applied to those who sat on the throne, it was otherwise immutable and irrevocable. The kings themselves supported a strong, well-respected legal mechanism, because—to the extent that trade relies upon trust between the buyer and the seller—the law was essential to the Persians' pursuit of commerce and large-scale agriculture. The Achaemenids, and Darius in particular, distinguished themselves by their devotion to the system.

Persians and foreigners alike called Darius the Lawgiver, a title that pleased him. "My law—of that they feel fear," said the inscription he chose for his tomb, "so that the stronger does not smite nor destroy the weak." Though this fragment provides a hint of Darius' dedication to the abstract function of law, and though there are frequent references in his own chronicles and other written sources to specific

Pomp and Protocol of the Regal Court

Because Persian society revered the institution of kingship as highly as it did, the king's public functions were conducted with pomp and great formality. The attitude comes through clearly in the relief on the left, a rare Achaemenid sculpture that captures the ceremony attending a monarch's performance of his office.

The carving, found in the treasury at Persepolis, exactly matches in size a panel on the façade of the audience hall, where delegates from subject nations offer gifts to the Great King (*pages 35-43*). Thus, archaeologists hold that the scene was made originally for the apadana and interpret the figure approaching the throne as chief of protocol, conferring with his majesty about arriving tribute bearers. Significantly, both ruler and crown prince are rendered larger than those around them, and a low dais raises them further above all others.

The enthroned monarch, probably Darius the Great, and his heir apparent receive in audience a court official, who touches hand to lips in a gesture of reverence. Behind the two regal personages—both wearing crowns and the long square-tipped beards that signify royalty—stand three personal attendants.

statutes, no actual code has ever been discovered. Without this hard evidence modern scholars have had to assemble the outlines of Persian law from a variety of non-legal sources, including the later books of the Old Testament, which describe times when the Promised Land was under Persian rule and refer repeatedly to the "law of the Medes and the Persians". In pursuing this analytical task, experts have come to believe that the Persians did not advance the underlying philosophy of law so much as they extended and developed the use of existing Middle Eastern legal concepts—which they generally practised in an impartial and efficient manner.

The law codes of the Middle East were first recorded about 1,000 years after the birth of writing itself. In ordering them to be compiled, early rulers were trying to systematize general custom within their society's overall moral framework. Thus solid precedent rather than theory was the basis for deciding every legal issue. The actual codification of law arranged the system of precedents in a logical order, and was a significant advance over the legal systems of preliterate times because in being written—on stone, on tablets or on some other durable material—it could be circulated to all parts of the community with a reasonable chance of being applied evenhandedly to everyone.

Naturally, therefore, scholars have paid close attention to the influence of such pre-Achaemenid legal thought on the Persian imperial law. Studying

A Persian (centre) and two Medes—probably high officials in the imperial bureaucracy—await a royal reception. The relief, from Xerxes' audience hall at Persepolis, was rendered with an informality and a sense of human communication that is rare in Achaemenid art; the Persian holds the hand of one Mede while engaging in conversation with the other.

fragments of a code drawn up by Hammurabi for the people of Babylonia around 1800 B.C., analysts have concluded that this document—actually a record inscribed on a black diorite stele and preserved in Susa—represents an ancestral form of the laws the Persians later disseminated throughout their whole empire.

Indeed, the language of Persian law seems to have been borrowed directly from the Babylonians. No sooner had Darius secured his throne in 521 B.C. than he was rendering judgments in phrases that appear to have been copied verbatim out of Hammurabi's 1,300-year-old casebooks. And Darius not only borrowed heavily from the Babylonian lawyer-king but also became a passionate spokesman, as Hammurabi had been, for the firm rule of law.

One of Darius' inscriptions bore the following declaration: "I am of such a character: What is right I love and what is not right I hate. . . . The man who decides for the Lie I hate. . . . And whoever injures, according to what he has injured I punish. . . . Of the man who speaks against the Truth, never do I trust a word." For the Persians, who regarded "the Truth" and "the Lie" as sacred definitions of good and evil, the law was held to be unalterable.

The Book of Esther relates that King Xerxes' advisors urged him to banish his queen, who had disobeyed his commands, lest "the great ladies of Persia and Media who have heard of the queen's behaviour" imitate her independence. The king's counsellors also recommended that the banishment order "be inscribed in the laws of the Persians and Medes, never to be revoked". Xerxes followed their advice, ordering all women in the empire to "give honour to their husbands high and low alike".

Another famous Biblical account deals with the prophet Daniel. At one time an important official in the satrapy of Babylonia, Daniel was held in high esteem by Darius. Yet he was thrown to the lions in their den as the result of a proceeding against him under the "law of the Medes and the Persians which stands forever". Enemies of Daniel—governors who were jealous of the favour shown him by Darius—had induced the monarch to publish a statute forbidding anyone to petition any god or man, except the king himself, for 30 days; they felt certain that Daniel's religious convictions would compel him to break the law. As they had expected, Daniel was caught praying. When Darius, "much distressed", tried to save his favourite from punishment, the assembled advisors reminded him "that by the law of the Medes and Persians, no ordinance or decree issued by the king may be altered". Darius dared not challenge their assertion, and Daniel was condemned to his punishment. (In the Biblical account, at any rate, the story ended happily; Daniel's god sent angels to calm the lions, and the condemned man was not even slightly injured. Overjoyed, the king had Daniel's accusers thrown to the lions in his place, and this time the lions tore the victims to pieces.)

Apart from the king and the lawgivers of his retinue, Persian justice was also dispensed through a system of courts, though little is known about how they worked. There probably were two courts functioning side by side in each jurisdiction: one sat on cases arising out of family, inheritance and property conflicts and referred to customary law in its judgments; the other was concerned with imposing and interpreting the king's law, which dealt with such state issues as taxation and transgressions committed

◄ This nine-foot stone figure—a unique four-winged guardian spirit—was carved in the Sixth Century B.C. on a doorjamb of the gatehouse at Pasargadae during the reign of Cyrus the Great. The sculpture is the oldest intact Achaemenid bas-relief yet found.

Supported by 30 columns set on square ► limestone plinths, the central hall of Cyrus' residential palace at Pasargadae covered an area of more than 7,000 square feet. The tower in the background, framed by the snow-covered Zagros Mountains, probably served a religious function.

against the government, its officers and its property.

Royal judges were appointed to serve for life or until they were disqualified for bad behaviour. Punishments were harsh; mutilation, impalement and crucifixion were common, and no penalties were more severe than those imposed on erring magistrates. Sisamnes, a royal Persian judge during Cambyses' reign, was caught accepting a bribe to fix a case. Cambyses ordered that Sisamnes' skin be removed in strips and thereafter used to upholster the judge's own courtroom chair. He then appointed Sisamnes' son to the same judicial post and told him to remember, when making decisions, where he was sitting and why he was there.

To transmit to the judges the new laws and regulations decreed in the king's court, the sovereign and his advisors most certainly called upon the services of one or more scribes. Since literacy was rare in Persia, scribes were among the most important functionaries in the king's service. The tongue most often spoken at the royal court was Old Persian, but the language of record, the lingua franca of business and diplomacy, was Aramaic. Scribes taking dictation in the king's tongue were expected to translate into Aramaic as they wrote. Fortunately for them, this language had a 22-letter alphabet and was immeasurably easier to write than the complex cuneiform script employed by earlier peoples. Furthermore, it could be written in ink on flexible leather or papyrus, rather than incised on clay tablets as cuneiform was. Hence the records themselves were incomparably more convenient to carry about, store and send over long distances.

Although reading and writing were not part of a prince's preparation for the throne, business-like

Persian kings seem to have been well aware of the value of good record keeping. The Book of Esther states that the execution of two eunuchs who threatened King Xerxes was "recorded in the royal chronicles in the presence of the king". In a later episode, the same Biblical account relates that Xerxes suffered one night from insomnia and called for a scribe to read some records to him. Roused from bed —or perhaps there was a secretary on standby duty all night—this scribe read to Xerxes from "the chronicle of daily events", which reminded the king that he had not yet rewarded a subordinate for informing him of a plot.

Another example of efficient filing shows how the Persian king could monitor the details of government in a distant conquered territory. During Darius' reign, Tattenai, the governor of the Babylonian sub-satrapy that included Jerusalem, was irked to find the Jews busily reconstructing their temple, which had been destroyed 68 years earlier by the Babylonians. Tattenai knew that he had not authorized the work himself. According to the Book of Ezra, the governor went to the site and challenged the elders to tell him who gave them permission to rebuild the temple. The Jewish leaders cited a proclamation that Cyrus had issued after his conquest of Babylon. The governor, doubting their word but unwilling to reject their story altogether for fear they might be right about the decree, immediately dispatched a letter to King Darius asking him to "let search be made in the royal archives there in Babylon" to see if the Jews were answering truthfully.

No record of Cyrus' decree existed in the Babylonian archives, but further investigation turned up a copy of the order filed away in another royal records storehouse at Ecbatana. After his predecessor's decree was read to him, Darius ordered Tattenai not only to "keep away from the place" but even to pay for the building "in full and from the royal funds accruing from the taxes".

In the normal course of events, such a direct dialogue between the king and the head of a small unit in the empire would have been rare. The main burden of day-to-day operations fell upon a hierarchy of bureaucrats led, from Darius' reign onwards, by a small group of Persian noblemen.

Since a conspiracy of nobles had given Darius the crown, it became axiomatic that without the active support of the aristocracy, any Achaemenid king would be hard pressed to maintain his position. With the successful outcome of his drive to power, a grateful Darius had elevated to special status the six peers who had helped kill his rival Gaumata; and in the Behistun inscriptions he called upon posterity to see to the welfare of their descendants. Ranked socially with the Achaemenids themselves, these nobles, along with the royal line, became the Seven Families, the most distinguished houses of Persia and the inner circle of the court. Oaths and ties of blood bound the families to the throne; after his coronation, Darius took his wives solely from this peerage and succeeding kings may have done the same.

Just below the members of the Seven Families was another elite category of hereditary landholders. Chief among these well-born associates were high-ranking military officers, important priests and government managers—men who oversaw the running of the imperial treasury, enforced the king's law, or carried out other administrative policies having to do with trade, irrigation and agriculture.

Rarely at court, but as important in the system as the court-based aristocracy, were the satraps, most of whom were drawn, during and after Darius' reign, from the ranks of the Seven Families as part of a conscious Persianization of the provinces. Under Darius, Persians even began to take over a larger share of the lesser posts under the satraps. Throughout the empire, colonies of Persians who staffed provincial chancelleries, filled judgeships, directed building projects, collected taxes and commanded military garrisons became as evident as communities of Englishmen would be in far corners of the British Empire more than 2,000 years later.

The Persian noblemen who filled all the top jobs in and out of court were tied to the king by a kind of feudal contract. Beneficiaries of royal largess in the form of land and other gifts, they were obligated to render the sovereign unquestioned personal loyalty and military service as officers; they were also required to supply troops that varied in number according to the amount of land the nobles held. Though they were exempt from the taxes that non-Persians paid, and though in the best of times the bond was a high honour and a lucrative station, this contractual obligation could be burdensome. Men so bound to the king were identified by the leather sword belts they wore about their waists. A man's failure to fulfil his contract to the king resulted in the cutting of his belt and, presumably, death.

Under the system, the king benefited by the fact that he could rely on pre-existing armies whenever he needed them—forces that he himself did not have to maintain. Also, revenue required for royal expenditures came from the spoils of war captured by those armies, as well as from taxes—in coin, precious metals, goods and labour—levied on the millions of

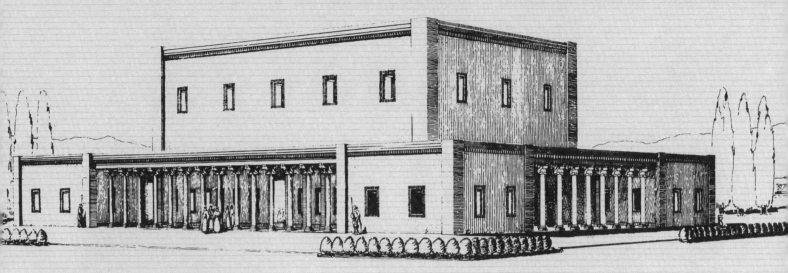

The 36-foot-tall central section of Cyrus' audience hall at Pasargadae, reconstructed in 1941 by architect-archaeologist Friedrich Krefter, was surrounded by colonnaded porticoes. Royal structures at this site were oblong; those built at Persepolis by Darius and his successors were square.

non-Persian subjects they brought under his rule.

Much of the revenue was spent on building a series of great royal capitals—a remarkable splurge of construction designed to enhance the king's own majesty and that of his empire. Before the Persian Empire fell, it had five part-time capitals. One of these, Pasargadae, was erected by Cyrus in celebration of his crucial victory over the Medes. Pasargadae's location in the home province of Persia (modern Fars), hundreds of miles east of the empire's economic and military centres, soon proved impractical for the daily conduct of imperial business. But the place had prestige as a national shrine and was graced with several elaborate structures, including a royal palace, an audience hall and the tomb of Cyrus himself. After Cyrus, Achaemenid kings went to Pasargadae to be crowned. As part of the coronation ceremony, they donned Cyrus' robes and ate a traditional nomad's meal of figs and sour milk. Otherwise, visits to Pasargadae were infrequent.

Cyrus also saw to the rebuilding of Babylon and used this ancient city as his capital when affairs of state brought him to the plains of Mesopotamia. Of the Babylonians, Cyrus declared: "The dishonouring yoke was removed from them. Their fallen dwellings I restored; I cleared out the ruins." As crown prince, Cyrus' son Cambyses preferred Babylon to other cities and lived there until after he ascended the throne, when he launched his military campaign in Egypt.

Darius, perhaps desiring a fresh start or a strategically better location, moved the empire's chief administrative offices from Babylon to Susa, the old Elamite capital. Susa stood at the hub of a network of roads and waterways, some 300 miles northwest of Pasargadae and 225 miles east of Babylon. Susa's populace had a long tradition of government service; in its time of glory under Elamite rule, the city had had as many as 5,400 men on the palace payroll.

Darius sought to expand Susa and build a capital worthy of his imperial successes. Work began in 521 B.C., while he was still battling insurgents within the empire. Judging from the extent of the ruins uncovered in recent decades, construction must have continued throughout his reign. Darius lavished colonnaded limestone palaces, halls and forts upon the city. The labourers and craftsmen he imported from all over his empire helped to make Susa as international in character as Babylon itself, and the Persian

This statue of Darius the Great, now headless, was sculptured in Egypt around 510 B.C. and shipped to the Persian capital at Susa. Unearthed in 1972, it stands nearly eight feet in its truncated state and weighs four tons. On the robe and pedestal, inscriptions in Egyptian hieroglyphs and in the cuneiform of three other Middle Eastern tongues extol this King of Kings.

kings made Susa rich with the store of treasure they brought as a consequence of conquest and taxes.

But the highland-bred Persians learned to dread Susa's intense midsummer heat. The Greek geographer Strabo said that a lizard venturing on to a Susa street at noon in summer would be cooked alive, and temperatures higher than 130° F. recorded there in modern times confirm his harsh view of the place. For relief in summer, the Achaemenid court first moved to higher country—to the old Median capital of Ecbatana in the Zagros Mountains. But while Darius and his successors were travelling around from country to country, they were also gathering ideas for the grandest and remotest of their royal residences: Persepolis, which would eventually become the climactic focus of Achaemenid building efforts (*pages 125-131*)—a dynastic centre where Darius and the later kings were buried.

The tendency of the court to keep moving among the capitals and, above all, the sprawling geography of the Persian realms required a swift and foolproof method of communication. Meeting this need was one of Darius' highest priorities, and it led to a striking innovation: the setting up of an empire-wide pony-express service for royal mail. Messages passing between Darius and his outlying governors, like Tattenai, were carried by relay riders on horses specially bred for speed. "There is nothing in the world that travels faster than these Persian couriers," Herodotus declared. He stated that there was one horse and rider for each day of the journey and that a message could be carried in seven days from Sardis in Lydia to Susa—a distance of 1,677 miles, which took three months for a caravan to cover.

Alexander, and later the Romans, adopted the system; and echoes of the Persian mail carriers' exemplary performance are found today in the slogan of the United States Postal Service. "Nothing," said Herodotus, "stops these couriers from covering their allotted stages in the quickest possible time—neither snow, rain, heat, nor darkness."

For short bulletins that demanded a quick response, such as news of a local uprising, the Persians' mounted postal system was complemented by signals that could be transmitted even more rapidly along chains of hilltop fire towers. Messages were probably blinkered in a visual code analogous to modern Morse —the signalmen presumably screening the fires in sequences that were intelligible to trained watchers at the next beacon. The fire tower signal relay system remained in use in Iran from Achaemenid times until the electric telegraph made it obsolete in the 19th Century A.D.

The communications network was tailor-made for the empire's provincial government organization; because they could send an order or an inquiry and get a reply quickly, the Achaemenids were able to retain control of their powerful satraps and participate in the making of local policies on a regular basis. By staying abreast of any sign of trouble in the provinces, the kings could head off the small problems— always threatening to become larger ones—that naturally plagued so immense and diverse a country.

Within the sprawling empire, some of the individual satrapies were themselves huge. All the former Egyptian Empire became just one satrapy; and a few others, like the one on the Mediterranean coast that included Ionia, were more than a thousand miles from Susa. Such enormous areas and distances posed obvious difficulties and the Persians adapted to meet them. Satrapal boundaries were often changed; countries and city-states were regrouped to suit new administrative or political needs, particularly when— as was frequently the case—one became too large for a single man to govern. Over the years the trend was towards smaller and more manageable political units; there probably were more satrapies at the end of the Persian Empire than the 20 that Cyrus originally organized and staffed.

The policy of naming Persians and Medes to run the satrapies and their minor offices sometimes had unexpected results. Appointed for indefinite terms, on occasion outlasting the reign of the king who had designated them, certain Persian satraps eventually gained enough power of their own to threaten the central government. At times they even managed to establish their positions as a hereditary right, thereby enabling them to pass their offices from father to son—as the king himself did.

Indeed, the provincial rulers lived royally. Cyrus had told his first satraps "imitate men", and many kept smaller-scale versions of the Great King's court, complete with cupbearers, harems and treasure houses. They were supported both by the vast estates they came to own in their assigned territories and by the substantial fraction of the taxes they were allowed to keep before passing the imperial share on to Susa. With their courts, they travelled from castle to palace to private *paridaisa*, the Persians' word for superbly tended gardens and hunting parks. Herodotus related that Tritantaechmes, the satrap of Babylonia, had an income of about five bushels of silver a day. Tritantaechmes owned 800 stallions and had 16,000 mares in his personal stable. He had so many dogs, presum-

Guardians of the Palace at Susa

Around 515 B.C., when the Persian Empire was in its heyday, Darius the Great built his palace at Susa. The old Elamite town was geographically at the centre of his realm and therefore ideally situated to serve as an administrative centre. To construct the magnificent royal complex, the monarch imported both building materials and workmen from all corners of his domain. Among the finest artisans were the Babylonians assigned to create the glazed-brick friezes that decorated the palace's façade, several of which have been reconstructed by French archaeologists from fragments found at the site. A clay tablet uncovered at Susa proclaims the king's pride in the architectural achievement. "A splendid work was ordered," Darius boasted, "very splendid did it turn out."

Part of a military procession that once guarded the approach to the palace, these life-sized warriors in richly ornamental robes wear the twisted headband typical of native Susians.

Sphinxes, 28 inches high, were among the images protecting the palace. The Babylonian-style crowns reflect the artisans' origin.

ably for hunting, that "four large villages" received tax exemption in return for feeding the animals.

Men with such tremendous power and wealth obviously needed watching. Darius devised an effective means to check on their activities. To every satrapal establishment, he appointed a treasurer and secretary directly responsible to the king. The treasurer saw to the final accounting of monies that poured into the satrap's coffers, and the secretary was the sharp-eyed conduit for correspondence between monarch and satrap. In addition, the satrap was investigated regularly by special roving officers known as "the king's ears"—powerful individuals who sometimes were accompanied by large detachments of Persian troops in case anyone challenged their authority. They often descended on a satrapal chancellery without any advance notice, pored over the account books, checked the balance in the treasury, examined records of lawsuits, and probably interviewed staff and public to satisfy themselves that the king's will was being obeyed by his viceroy.

But perhaps the major counterweights to an overambitious satrap were the military garrisons stationed throughout the empire. The satrap was nominally the supreme military commander of his area, and in wartime the garrison's troops might be incorporated in a force under the satrap's leadership. Normally, however, garrison commanders were responsible directly to the Great King himself through a separate chain of command that bypassed the provincial governor. Satraps and subject peoples contemplating escape from Persian rule and taxes had only to glance over their shoulders at the local garrison of tough, disciplined soldiers to reconsider the matter.

This carefully balanced network of informants and armed policemen, constantly in touch with the king, enabled the Achaemenids to move quickly against those who offended the throne. The system's effectiveness was demonstrated in Darius' dealings with a Persian named Oroetes, satrap of Sardis, who conducted himself in a threateningly independent manner. Among other things. Oroetes had been noticeably derelict in coming to Darius' aid during the first stormy years of the king's reign. Further, he was said to have murdered another satrap and one of the king's own couriers. Oroetes had a personal bodyguard of 1,000 Persians, which suggests that he may have felt invulnerable to any pressures short of superior military force. If so, he was mistaken.

Darius—who, according to Herodotus, believed that "force is always beside the point when subtlety will serve"—brought the satrap to heel by sending just one man. This single officer carried a number of documents bearing the king's seal. At Oroetes' court, in the presence of the satrap's bodyguard, he handed over the letters one at a time to be read aloud by the royal secretary attached to Oroetes' staff. While the secretary read the first letter, an innocuous administrative order, the officer eyed the assembled soldiers to gauge their reaction. He saw "that they regarded the documents with respect—and, still more, the words they heard read from them". So he then passed to the royal secretary a letter that ordered the soldiers to cease serving Oroetes. On hearing it, they laid down their spears. Finally, the secretary delivered the last message: "King Darius commands the Persians in Sardis to kill Oroetes." Without hesitation the guards drew their swords and obeyed.

Despite such unquestioning loyalty of the army to

the king, the combat effectiveness of the army itself deteriorated as the tide of empire submerged more and greater varieties of people. Almost from the beginning, custom decreed that all men up to the age of 50 had an obligation to serve their country as royal warriors; a Persian boy's training from early childhood was directed to that end. There are no Persian documents that provide details of this martial preparation, but many Greek chroniclers reported on the training with admiration.

Xenophon, in his biography of Cyrus the Great, wrote that from the age of five or six until 15, a boy was introduced to the disciplines of riding, shooting arrows, and fighting on foot and on horseback. Strabo, the geographer, added that as a foretaste of army life boys were taught in groups of 50—with those of noble birth appointed nominal officers—and that they were given a taste for competition through gruelling cross-country foot races. The youngsters were also trained to endure extreme temperatures and to scavenge for their own provisions. At about age 20, the recruits were presumably ready to take their places in the king's standing army, where many of them remained until retirement.

Boys from prominent Persian families received, in addition to the general military training, preparation for their future roles as satraps, judges and royal officers. This schooling included drill in the heroic history of their ancestors, exposure to the workings of the court and the king's law—particularly in the discipline of truth-speaking—and instruction in beliefs and practices of the court religion.

In return for service to the king, young men of the upper class were rewarded with land, the profits from which became their pay. Persians of all ranks were repaid for distinguished service with symbolic honours, which included titles, family crests and divisional badges of triumph.

The professional core of the military was the famed Ten Thousand Immortals. One thousand of their number made up the elite royal bodyguard; in the later years of the empire their commander, or *hazarapatish*, doubled as the king's prime minister.

The table of organization for the army was established on the same basic unit of 50 used in training Persian boys. Typical elements contained 50 archers, 50 spearmen, 50 light or heavy cavalrymen. Within the basic unit were 10 five-man squads, each under a *pascadasapati*, the equivalent of a corporal. Two 50-man platoons made up a *drafsha*, or flag, presumably named for the standard they carried into battle. Because of the intensive training given Persian troops at all levels, even larger forces—such as the entire Immortals division of 10,000—were remarkably mobile and responsive, as Cyrus' lightning campaigns against Lydia and Babylonia demonstrated.

It was a very efficient system, at least in the early phases of the empire. Later, under such kings as Xerxes and Artaxerxes I, the throne was to rely increasingly on forces composed of draftees from the satrapies, and their record was less impressive; in effect, the expansion of imperial territory provided more manpower but brought about a reduction in its quality and patriotic fervour. Armed with a wide diversity of weapons, and fighting according to locally derived techniques and skills, these polyglot Persian armies also lost much of their manoeuvrability.

Instead of fielding hardened soldiers, the Persian vassals filled their troop levies with odds and sods. Xenophon scoffed: "Now the rulers make knights out of porters, bakers, cooks, cupbearers, bathroom attendants, butlers, waiters, chamberlains who assist them in retiring at night and in rising in the morning, and beauty-doctors who pencil their eyes and rouge their cheeks . . . these are the sort that they make into knights to serve for pay for them."

The multi-national armies that served the later kings were sorted according to function and nationality. Among the infantry were Persians in tunics and scale armour, turbaned Cissians, Scythians in tall pointed hats, Assyrians wearing bronze helmets, and phalanxes of Greek mercenaries who marched as a moving wall of shields and spears. They fought alongside Indians, Egyptians, Libyans, Bactrians and others in their equally distinctive garb. Mobile troops included camel-mounted Arabs, Persians astride armour-clad horses and squadrons of Persian war chariots equipped with viciously sharp scythes that projected from their wheels and sides and were capable of slashing through deep-ranked bodies of men.

In addition to such land forces, the Achaemenids supported a naval arm. They had made the acquisition of such maritime kingdoms as Phoenicia, Ionia and Egypt one of their early goals, and special allowances were offered to these states in exchange for transporting the Persian armies and fighting the empire's sea battles. Unlike all other subject states, the maritime cities in Phoenicia and Ionia were free to control their own internal affairs and were allowed to coin their own money.

Nevertheless, for all the success of their system, the Persians were to discover that the tendency of large administrative structures, embodying many interlocking and occasionally conflicting parts, is towards rigidity and cumbrousness. Not the least of the Achaemenids' achievements, however, was their ability to resist such atrophy for a remarkably long time. The results, for the majority of the empire's subjects, were benefits that went far beyond the functional technicalities of effective administration. Chief among these returns was a commerce of great diversity and liveliness. Indeed, as it turned out, what was good for the king and the people was also very good for business.

Royal Routines at Five Busy Capitals

Travelling between residences, a royal caravan moves through a mountain pass. Ruler and entourage ride inside the covered wagons.

To accommodate a complex imperial life, the Achaemenid kings had not one but five residences. Susa and Babylon, both ancient cities that predated the empire, were administrative centres; Pasargadae, founded by Cyrus the Great, was the site of coronations; Ecbatana, 6,000 feet above sea level, was a summer retreat; and Persepolis was the setting for the all-important New Year's celebration.

The king spent time holding court at each palatial complex. But even when he was absent, the cities bustled with activity. New construction was usually under way, including refinements to the palace, the apadana or the banquet hall—royal edifices built in the grandiose style of the Achaemenid rulers. And all the while, money was steadily flowing into or being doled out of the imperial treasuries.

The scenes reconstructed on these pages are based on evidence at Persepolis—the supreme example of the Persians' architectural style, wealth and regal pomp.

Monumental Works in Constant Progress

Near a royal residence, labourers quarry sandstone or limestone for construction by carving rectangular blocks from living rock. First, deep parallel trenches are dug and holes are bored in perpendicular rows. Into the holes workmen drive foot-long wedges and soak them with water, causing the wood to swell and split the rock. Finally, the wedge-and-water process is repeated in the trench bottoms to free each block from the rock bed. At the rear, several men are shaping a large piece of extracted stone into a column segment.

Overseen by two royal inspectors (left), hoisters strain with stout ropes and wedges to right a 23-ton column segment, or drum, on to a fluted base—the stone having first been hauled up a solid ramp of mud brick with a protective covering of wooden slats, half hidden at right. Since the upper sections of the columns were several tons lighter than the lower ones, they could be hoisted in the air by blocks and tackles above drums already standing and then lowered into position, as is being done in the scaffolding at rear.

A Steady Flow of Wealth through the Treasury

Construction labourers—quarriers, stone haulers, carvers and woodworkers—queue up with smiths and other artisans to be paid by a royal treasurer. Women, including goldsmiths from the satrapy of Caria, are not present; though their earnings were high, their menfolk collected payment for them. The average wage was about one silver shekel a month, but the sum was rarely delivered in currency. Instead, a fixed rate of equivalents in livestock or drink was used: one sheep was worth three shekels, one jug of wine or oil, one shekel.

Inside a well-filled treasury building, the comptroller—wearing a tall hat—calls out the measures of wealth passing before him. Two scribes record the amounts, one on a parchment scroll, the other on a clay tablet. The revenue in taxes and tributes included coins, vessels and ornaments of silver and gold—all appraised against standard pyramidal stone weights. The objects were often melted down and the metal poured into standard-sized moulds to form ingots, which could be minted into currency when the king gave the order.

For Honoured Guests, a Prized Audience

Delegations of emissaries or supplicants seeking an audience with the king pass into a gatehouse through a huge portal; the wooden doors are decorated with bronze reliefs. The visitors were expected to remain here until summoned by an usher to the apadana, or audience hall, which was a separate building. When the announcement was made that the monarch was ready, the dignitaries entered the hall and approached the empty throne; after another interval, the king ceremoniously entered by a side door to greet his guests.

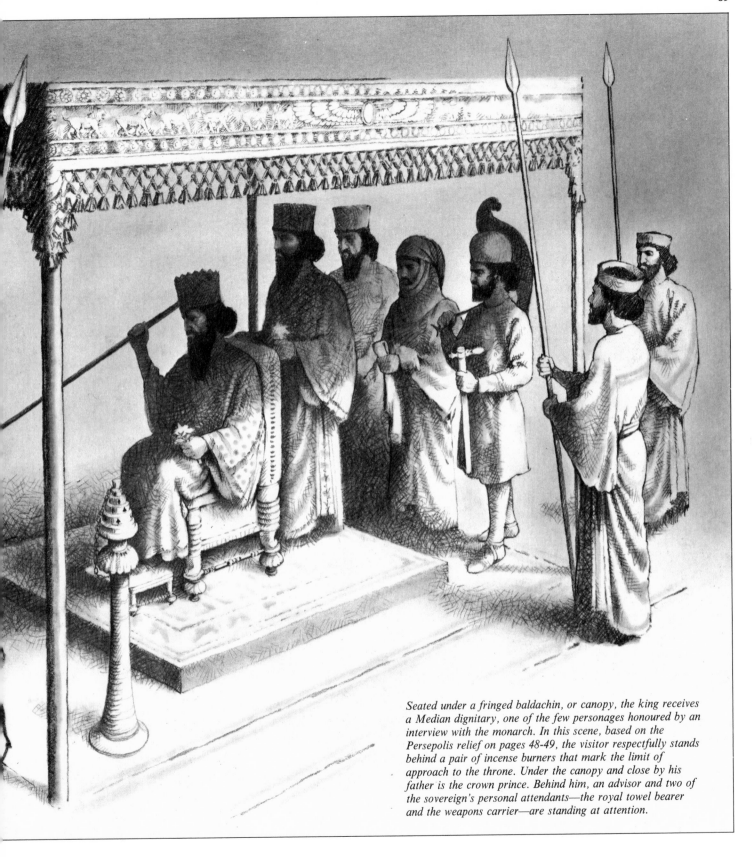

Seated under a fringed baldachin, or canopy, the king receives a Median dignitary, one of the few personages honoured by an interview with the monarch. In this scene, based on the Persepolis relief on pages 48-49, the visitor respectfully stands behind a pair of incense burners that mark the limit of approach to the throne. Under the canopy and close by his father is the crown prince. Behind him, an advisor and two of the sovereign's personal attendants—the royal towel bearer and the weapons carrier—are standing at attention.

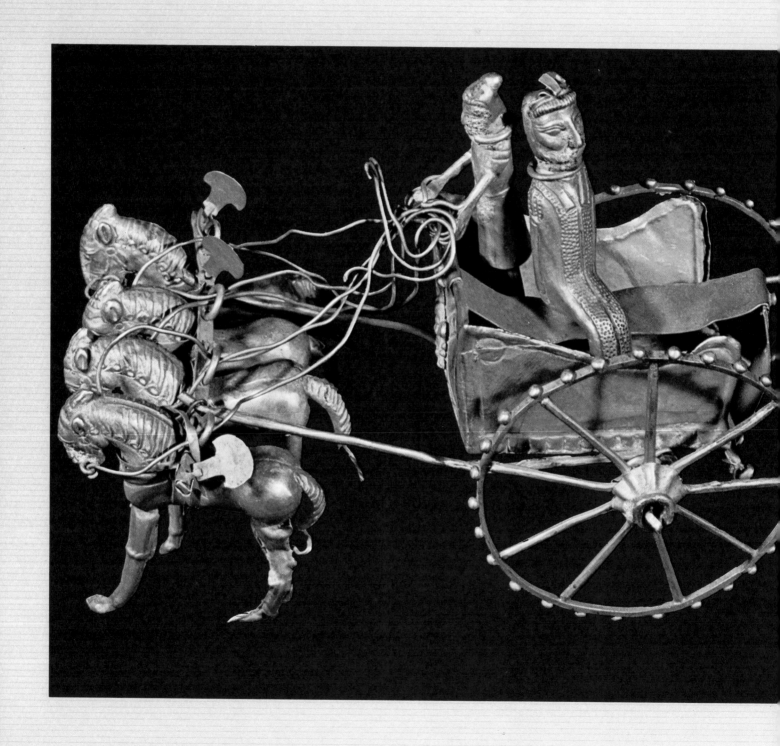

The Persian people called Cyrus a father, Cambyses a tyrant and Darius a merchant. For the Persians, the term merchant—or tradesman—was not one of opprobrium but of admiration, a tribute to Darius' ability to create the healthy economy that was to be a pillar of his reign. And though in time the booming economy he promoted failed, largely through inflation, for half a century all parts of the empire shared in unprecedented prosperity.

To achieve and maintain this happy state of affairs, Darius initiated programmes that reached into every aspect of his subjects' lives: he systematized taxation; standardized weights, measures and monetary units to simplify commercial exchange; improved and extended transportation networks, including roads and an early version of the Suez Canal; developed a royal merchant marine; patronized agriculture, which was the foundation of Persia's internal economy; encouraged the growth of a banking system; and promoted international trade. The results, as Darius had foreseen, not only raised the level of gold ingots in his vaults but also increased the standard of living of the entire Middle East.

Taxation reform was the first of his innovations to bear positive fruit. When he ascended the throne in 522 B.C., the empire's system of taxes was a haphazard structure. Taxes were collected irregularly, applied inconsistently from one community to another, and based upon presumptions of income that

Travelling on business, Persian nobles rode in chariots resembling this gold model from the Fifth or Fourth Century B.C. *The passenger sat with his back to the driver, who stood while controlling the four-horse team. The miniature is less than four inches long and is part of the Oxus Treasure, a hoard of artifacts—mostly Persian—found in Afghanistan.*

often bore no relation to the actual wealth of the taxpayers. In Mesopotamia, for instance, assessors decided what a farmer should pay before his harvest was in. If his crop—palm dates or grain or whatever it might be—later failed, he nonetheless had to pay the full predetermined tax.

Darius continued Cyrus' practice of exempting native Persians from all taxes, but he did set about putting an end to inequities in other parts of his realm. About 520 B.C., he ordered officials in every Persian satrapy to measure the agricultural lands and calculate their average per annum yields. The figures were then used to determine how much each landholder should pay in produce or money to the satrapy's tax collectors and, thus, how much revenue each satrapy should remit to the royal treasury.

Taxes on agricultural produce in Darius' time might have amounted to roughly 20 per cent of the value of a given estate's crop. Other industries—fishing, mining, textile and clothing manufacture—were similarly assessed. In each satrapy, a share of the total revenue collected was skimmed off by the local governor as food allowance, a generous sum with which he ran his own vice-regal court; the rest was shipped off to the treasury at Susa to be counted, recorded and stored.

According to Herodotus, who compiled much information on the Persians' taxation system under Darius, the most common forms of payment were precious metals apportioned in basic units of weight. The largest unit, the talent, had been in general use throughout the ancient world for more than 2,000 years, though it varied somewhat from country to country. The Persian talent weighed about 66 pounds and was commonly cast as a disc or an oval. Its buying power was enormous; a talent of silver was worth about £1,050 in modern currency, and a half talent would pay the entire 200-man crew of an oared warship for a month. A gold talent was worth approximately 13 times as much as one of silver.

The original meaning of the word "talent" in the language of the Babylonians, who popularized its use, was "burden", suggesting that its weight was related to the load an able-bodied man could carry over a long distance. That image, however, conveys an inaccurate impression of convenience; actually, the talent was so large and of such high value that it was useful only in major transactions—such as those between states and satrapies. Smaller denominations, also measured by weight, had wider circulation. The talent was subdivided into 60 minas and the mina into 60 shekels or 100 drachmas, each drachma weighing just one-seventh of an ounce.

Satrapal taxes were often paid—or at least reckoned—in talents and, Herodotus reported, by far the largest contributor to the royal storehouse each year was the satrapy of India. "The Indians, the most populous in the known world," the Greek historian wrote, "paid the largest sum: 360 talents of gold dust." Those gold talents, if converted to silver—the more common medium of payment in many satrapies—would have come to just under 5,000 talents of silver or about 330,000 pounds of the metal. Babylonia, the second largest contributor, was annually assessed 1,000 silver talents; Egypt, 700 silver talents; the Medes, 450 silver talents. All told, Darius collected nearly 15,000 talents of silver a year.

In addition to such revenue in precious metals, the empire's treasury was enriched by assessments in goods and services. The Arabs, for instance, could be counted on annually for more than 6,600 pounds of frankincense, a fragrant, resinous product of tropical and subtropical trees. The Egyptians were obliged to provide 120,000 bushels of grain, the Kushites 200 logs of ebony and 20 elephant tusks. And Babylonia paid a grim annual tribute of 500 castrated boys, who were then sent off to the Persian court to serve as eunuchs in the king's household. Beyond all these regular levies, there were harbour and market tariffs, road tolls, and duties on domesticated animals and various other highly profitable enterprises.

But transferring actual goods was cumbersome, and dealing in large volumes of precious metals was downright risky. Any exchange in talents required not only a scale to determine the value of the sum changing hands but also, if the integrity of the metal was in doubt—as it often was—a test for purity. To assay metal purported to be gold, the ingot was melted in a complex process that revealed how much of it was pure; a quicker but less reliable test was to rub the alleged gold over a black touchstone—a very hard rock resembling flint that could be marked by softer substances—and then to judge the colour of the smudge produced on the stone. It took much expertise and equipment to conclude any honest deal.

It was, therefore, one of Darius' major contributions that, from his time onwards, government officials—and to a lesser extent the general populace—had a convenient alternative to bulk exchanges: a standard imperial coinage. What distinguished coins from the various other units of exchange that the Middle East most commonly used in business was that the currency came from one source: the government, which guaranteed its worth. Previously, any citizen could assemble quantities of precious metal and melt

This gold daric bears the portrait of an Achaemenid king, idealized as a warrior. The coin, measuring less than an inch across, was minted around 330 B.C., just before Greek forces defeated Persia. Ironically, encroaching Greek influence is distinctly reflected in the stylish drape of the monarch's robe.

it into a unit of weight—a talent, a mina or a shekel; but now only the state could issue coins. Further, the royal mint scrupulously supervised their manufacture, assuring not only their conformity but also the purity of their metallic content. It followed logically that while an ingot made under no such controls was always subject to doubt—it might contain cheap metals or even stones under a precious exterior—a coin could be accepted at its face value. Of course, coinage could be counterfeited, but the Persians discouraged forgeries by imposing death as punishment.

The Persians did not invent coinage; fittingly enough, Croesus, the notoriously rich king of Lydia, is accorded the honour of conceiving the idea. But the Persians are given a large share of the credit for having legitimized the use of coins throughout much of the ancient world, especially in Asia. It was Darius' genius to recognize that Croesus' invention would further his own empire: by surmounting the obstacle to international trade posed by differing local monetary values, the new system would encourage disparate peoples to do business with one another; active and conveniently transacted commerce would stimulate widespread communication; and all this expansionist activity could be easily monitored by the royal court itself.

The new standard was the daric, so named either for the king himself or, more likely, for the Old Persian word meaning gold: *dari*. The coin, just under three-quarters of an inch in diameter, weighed one-third of an ounce and was 98 per cent pure gold; the other 2 per cent was an alloy of silver and other metals added to harden the coin. (Its particular unit value, some historians have suggested, was equal to the generally accepted worth of a healthy, mature ox, in earlier times a convenient standard by which pastoral peoples were able to appraise other goods.)

Darius also inaugurated the sigloi, less valuable coins minted of 90 per cent pure silver and 10 per cent alloy; they measured about three-quarters of an inch in diameter and weighed about one-fifth of an ounce. Twenty sigloi equalled one daric.

The minting of darics was a right reserved solely for the throne. But the coining of silver sigloi was permitted in the outlying satrapies. The sigloi differed somewhat from region to region and, to that extent, the practice compromised the uniformity of the imperial coinage. As a result, imperial tax collectors usually ignored the face value of all but the royal sigloi, accepting those minted elsewhere only by weight and often discounting them heavily and unfairly. Nevertheless, by such measures Darius and his successors were able to keep their currency from significant debasement until the empire's decline.

However innovative the idea of uniform government coinage, the mechanism was somewhat clumsy. The coins did not circulate until they were worn out; the average time span for any one daric was probably rather short. Many darics were scarcely delivered from the mint before they were earmarked for the payment of someone's taxes and sent back to the royal treasuries. There they were melted down and poured into earthenware crocks. When the metal hardened, the crock was broken away, leaving ingots, which were easier to store than coins. Moreover, the tax revenues of the state were so enormous that the portion of collections that might be needed for disbursement at any one time was only a small percentage of the total on hand. But when there was a campaign to be fought, a foreign monarch to be bribed or a public-works project to be funded, the ingots were remelted and new coins were struck.

Some darics went back into circulation to pay the gangs of labourers who constructed and improved the empire's roads and waterways. Designed to strengthen the empire's military effectiveness by shortening the time required to move armies and military supplies, these communications links inevitably served the cause of commerce as well; they enabled traders and their goods to travel long distances more quickly and more safely than ever before.

Cyrus, who had initiated the mounted royal courier system to keep in touch with his satraps and generals, probably also began construction of the road system that the couriers used. But it was Darius who carried through the massive project. Before the Achaemenids, many roads had been little more than crude caravan trails between one island of civilized life and another. They spanned vast wildernesses infested with marauders and thieves; only a foolhardy or unusually courageous merchant would journey along such a track without a well-armed escort.

Darius' engineers turned these perilous routes into linear extensions of civilization, straightening and smoothing them, laying rudimentary paving across marshland and, in some places, cutting ruts to the standard axle width of chariots and wagons to help keep the vehicles on the highway.

The principal route was the Royal Road, which ran more than 1,600 miles from the imperial residence at Susa to the old Lydian capital of Sardis—in Darius' time the chief centre of Persian administration for western Asia Minor. The most heavily travelled of Darius' highways, the Royal Road was maintained by a small army of civilian and military personnel. Along its length there were, Herodotus noted, four ferry crossings, four heavily guarded checkpoints (at least two with gates), scores of courier relay stations and no fewer than 111 inns that—in the fashion of a modern guidebook compiler awarding stars or crossed forks—the Greek historian rated "excellent".

Those travelling on foot could expect to take about 90 days to go the distance; and the inns were situated so that, barring bad weather or some other occurrence, the distance from one night's lodging to the next could easily be covered without fatigue. On relatively flat terrain, the Persian planners estimated, a day's walk would be about five parasangs, or 18 miles. Where the terrain was rougher, as in the stretch that went up and over the mountains between Susa and Erbil, inns were somewhat closer together —about four parasangs apart.

Other major arteries reached east across the Iranian plateau from Ecbatana to Bactria and India, and west through Palestine to Egypt. Though no inns were set up on these roads, one—the route to Egypt— had water caches along the stretch that led through the Sinai desert, to alleviate the problem of thirst that had hitherto plagued travellers. The road's builders commandeered quantities of empty earthenware jugs that had held Phoenician and Greek wine im-

ported into Egypt, and refilled them with water. The jugs were then stored underground in the desert at frequent intervals along the road.

While Darius' far-ranging road projects were politically and commercially prudent, his development of new water routes was truly adventurous. Never before had so many riverboats and seaworthy ships traversed Middle Eastern waterways, which Darius actually augmented. One of his most spectacular achievements in expanding maritime activity was the construction of an early version of the Suez Canal, a channel that ran northwards from the Gulf of Suez to a point where it joined the Pelusiac branch of the Nile and connected with the Mediterranean.

Work on the canal had been begun by an Egyptian pharaoh a century earlier, around 600 B.C., as a means of opening an east-west trade channel to the Red Sea from major commercial centres in the Nile Valley; but the project was abandoned, unfinished, after it had cost the lives of 120,000 workmen. In 500 B.C., Darius' engineers and thousands of shovel-wielding subjects resumed the effort. To provide an outlet to the Mediterranean, the Persians altered the course of the canal to run roughly north-south and dug an artificial watercourse more than 90 miles long and 150 feet wide; including the natural waterway through the Bitter Lakes in Sinai, the entire channel extended 125 miles.

Great ceremony evidently attended the canal's official opening, which probably took place soon after 500 B.C. Five massive granite markers were erected along the canal's banks in honour of the magnificent feat of engineering. An inscription on one of the surviving monuments proclaims: "Says Darius the King: I am a Persian. . . . I gave the order to dig this canal from a river by the name Nile which flows in Egypt, to the sea which goes from Persia." Other inscriptions also report that among the first vessels to pass through were 24 ships bound from Memphis for Persia laden with tribute from the Egyptian satrapy.

Meanwhile, Darius was energetically sponsoring exploratory sea voyages to regions beyond the margins of his existing territory. One expedition, dispatched to reconnoitre the Greek coastline in preparation for an invasion that Darius was planning, sailed in three ships under the guidance of Democedes, an Italian with extensive experience in Greece. After the party had explored parts of the coast and offshore islands, Democedes, who was homesick, persuaded the Persians accompanying him to sail on to Italy, where he jumped ship. But although all the Persian vessels were lost, numerous survivors managed to get home and report to the king.

The voyage was notable for two reasons: first, although the Achaemenids had heard about Greece from such arriving travellers as Democedes, no Persian had heretofore seen the place and reported on it first-hand; and second, because the reconnaissance was effective—the first step in the initial Persian assault, launched in 517 B.C., on the Greek islands.

Another naval expedition sponsored by Darius was commanded by Scylax, an Ionian navigator from the newly subjugated territories on Asia Minor's west coast. The voyage began with an overland journey. The party travelled across the Iranian plateau all the way to the headwaters of India's river Indus, then boarded ship and sailed down the Indus to open water, west on the Indian Ocean, and northwest through the Red Sea. The vessel reached Suez, the entrance to the canal, at the end of a two-and-a-half-year voyage. Scylax reported fully to the court on the fabulous wealth of western India—the areas east of Bactria that were then outside Persian dominion. Thereafter, partly thanks to Scylax' expedition, Darius felt confident about sending an army to take over the lands between Bactria and the Indus. After 500 B.C., ships in the Persians' service were making regular runs to northwestern India and returning with pearls, tortoise shells and spices.

King Xerxes, Darius' successor, also supported exploration—but with little profit. He sent his cousin Sataspes to sea with orders to circumnavigate Africa. Sataspes did not relish the assignment, but it was the better of two bad choices. If he refused to go, Xerxes threatened to put him to death for raping a noblewoman. So Sataspes set forth from Egypt and sailed westwards through the Mediterranean and then down Africa's Atlantic coast. But he never rounded the Cape of Good Hope. How far south he did get is uncertain, but after some months he despaired of ever reaching the Red Sea, because—he claimed—lack of wind prevented his ship from sailing any farther. He turned north again and retracing his course reached home, where he reported his failure to the king. Sceptical of the lame excuse given by his kinsman and angry at having been disobeyed, Xerxes had the feckless Sataspes impaled after all.

In their construction and acquisition of ships for such exploratory forays and for trade, the Persians followed their custom of borrowing or adapting the designs of other peoples. It seems certain that Persia's mariners sailed in ships modelled after those of the Phoenicians and Greeks. Propelled primarily by a single square sail, the merchant ships in the Persian fleet were built to greater length and beam than ever before to accommodate the first long-distance maritime trade in bulk goods. Craft capable of transporting 130 tons of freight were a familiar sight in ports all over the eastern Mediterranean and the Red Sea, and others with cargo capacities of up to 250 tons also plied the waterways.

Such vessels, and countless overland caravans, turned the ancient world into a common market. The spices of India, purple dye from Phoenicia, copper and silver from the mines of Anatolia, Egyptian glass, frankincense and myrrh from Arabia, timber from Asia Minor, Crete and Lebanon, as well as precious stones, weapons and art objects from all these places, were shuttled thousands of miles from their sources to consumers. Even quite commonplace products, such as wine, dried fish, oil, honey, furniture, inexpensive textiles and grain could now earn their freight costs and still turn a tidy profit for the merchants—also producing a tax for the king.

While trade boomed, carefully managed agriculture provided the real basis of the empire's well-being. The support of farming was not only a concern for government policy makers; agriculture, especially animal husbandry, was also a specific moral virtue in the Persians' religion.

Routine farming was promoted, but so was experimentation. Around 495 B.C. Darius wrote to Gadates, an official of Ionia, to censure him for interfering with the local management of a shrine to Apollo—but the king tempered his disapprobation with high compliments on the official's agricultural successes: "For in that you are cultivating my land, introducing food-crops from beyond the Euphrates...I commend your policy, and for this great credit will be given you in the house of the king."

Innovators like Gadates were rewarded with land and other riches. Meanwhile, royal agents were constantly dispatched to the satraps carrying new seeds for local farmers to plant in their fields. Alfalfa, naturally abundant in Media, was successfully planted in Greece to provide more nutritious forage for Persian army horses there; the animals had formerly been restricted to a diet of hay. The Persians introduced rice into Mesopotamia, pistachio nuts into Syria and sesame into Egypt. In Babylonia, the Persians encouraged the cultivation of flax for the manufacture of linen; though known there for more than a millennium, the plant had probably been used primarily as a source of oil, not as a fibre for weaving cloth.

Crop experimentation alone was not enough, however, to raise agricultural productivity to the ambitious levels demanded by the needs of an expanding empire. Particularly in the Persian homelands, where rainfall on the arid Iranian plateau rarely exceeded eight inches per year—and sometimes yielded as little as four inches—irrigation was essential to the maintenance of almost any form of farming. But the Persians were also at pains to extend artificial watering methods to the relatively fertile areas of conquered Mesopotamia, particularly in Babylonia.

In the Iranian interior the agricultural engineers faced a formidable obstacle: surface water in and near potentially arable land was inadequate for irrigation, and the Persians lacked the technological ability to locate deep subterranean water. They had no choice but to transport water by aqueducts from the mountains, where springs and freshets abounded. But because the precious liquid would have evaporated rapidly if carried in open channels under Persia's cloudless skies, the engineers had to adopt an ambitious, costly system of underground delivery called the *qanat*.

The *qanat* consisted of a slightly inclined tunnel that ran, sometimes for many miles, from a water source to a lower farming community. Along the *qanat*'s route, shafts were sunk at regular intervals to meet the tunnel. During construction, the shafts were used to remove earth and provide ventilation for the diggers; once the tunnel was finished, the shafts served as entries for inspectors who saw to the *qanat*'s maintenance.

The basic technology of the *qanat* had originally been developed not for irrigation but for mining, and credit for the invention must go not to the Persians but to some more ancient community—probably the Urartians. But the Persians had the manpower and the incentive to perfect the use of the tunnels for irrigation, and they introduced the *qanat* throughout the dry regions of their empire, from India to Egypt. Even today some of these works remain the principal water source in certain remote communities.

During the Fifth Century B.C., the Persians also greatly expanded the ancient irrigation canal system, by which the Babylonians had harnessed the Tigris and Euphrates rivers ever since the Fourth Millennium B.C. The whole of Babylonia was crisscrossed by channels that connected the two great rivers and spread their richly silted waters to every corner of the fertile flood plain.

This continuous infusion of moisture into the naturally rich alluvial soil made Babylonia the garden of the Persian Empire. The land was so productive that Herodotus was cautious in describing it, for fear the truth would be doubted. "The blades of wheat and barley are at least three inches wide," he reported. "As for millet and sesame, I will not say to what astonishing size they grow, though I know well enough; but I also know that people who have not been to Babylonia have refused to believe even what I have said already about its fertility."

An even bigger money-maker than grain for Babylonian farmers—and, through tax collectors, for the royal Persian treasury—was the date palm. A grove of palms was taxed at twice the rate of an equally large grainfield—because, as Herodotus noted, the generous palm fruit "supplies them with food, wine and honey". The tree's leaves also provided materials for basketry and fuel; the fruit stalks, fibre for rope-making; and finally, when the tree was no longer productive, its trunk was used in construction.

Theoretically, all the land belonged to the monarch and was held only in fee by his subjects. Under the earlier kings, this feudal contract obligated the fief-holder to set aside revenue for the equipment of troops, who were to be held in readiness for royal service. Thus, during Darius' reign fiefdoms were parcelled out in measures proportional to the individual's military obligations: "bow land", an area about 500 yards square, required payment for the services of an archer; a larger tract of "horse land" was expected to furnish the money for a mounted soldier; "chariot land" was a still larger parcel whose value was equated with the expense of supporting a war chariot, a driver and from two to four horses.

Text continued on page 82

Rare Personal Vignettes of Persian Life

This impression from a seal bearing the name of Darius the Great in the Persian, Elamite and Babylonian languages presents the chariot-borne king hunting lions beneath a winged symbol of his god, Ahuramazda. The agate seal (left) probably belonged to one of Darius' highest officials.

Persian treasury officials used cylinder seals, usually about one and a quarter inches high, to sign documents written on clay tablets; the instruments usually bore pictures like those on this and the following pages. The images, taken from seals made by craftsmen in Persia and Asia Minor during the Fifth or Fourth Century B.C., provide valuable insights into the daily pre-occupations of the Persians —revealed in scenes of gods, kings, nobles, warriors and, occasionally, the general populace.

The miniature engravings were excised on tubular pieces of semi-precious stone—often agate or chalcedony—which were rolled across the still-moist clay to produce the signatures. The high quality of the materials used indicates that the seals may have served their owners not merely as authenticating devices but as jewellery.

In the two battle scenes above—separated by the vertical line at left centre—the same Persian warrior tramples fallen foes and then spears others. In both panels of the seal, the god Ahuramazda hovers near by. To cut these intricate patterns on hard stone, bronze engraving tools were used.

The common people of Achaemenid times seldom appear on seals. In the case of the man shown here ploughing with his oxen, the fact that the Persians' religion sanctified farming may explain why such a homely chore was the chosen subject.

In this impression, Ahuramazda spreads his wings above a sacred fire tended by two royal figures. The difficult task of engraving ritual tableaux like this one was accomplished by artisans said to have spent five years in apprenticeship.

Dramatizing the chase, this view pits a dismounted hunter against a wild boar. Poised to protect his horse, the man attacks with a spear, and also holds what appears to be a cape —possibly a means of distracting the enraged tusker.

To vaunt his power, a Persian king, armed only with a dagger, was sometimes shown, as at left, combating a winged monster. A relief with the same motif appears on the palace of Darius I at Persepolis (page 30). The palm tree beside the crescent moon may be an emblem for royalty, and the prancing ibex is a traditional Iranian symbol for life and vigour.

A rare representation of Persian women, this imprint captures a moment in the royal harem. Surveyed by a crowned lady, standing next to the incense burner at right centre, a girl presents a bird to an enthroned queen or goddess.

The scheme was somewhat cumbersome, however; as time passed, the crown more and more frequently exacted cash rents instead of requiring troop levies from landholders—except in emergencies.

The holders of these fiefdoms were military or civil officers, noble families and sometimes institutions or large groups such as temples or military garrisons. Many of the estates were territorially enormous, embracing thousands of acres. Except for the need to pay the crown's fees and taxes in coin, the estates could be closed, self-sustaining economies. To raise cash, they had to sell at least part of their agricultural or manufactured products outside their boundaries—a requirement that stimulated the economy.

The labour of producing such agricultural wealth was performed throughout most of the empire by a lower class of field hands and artisans: free labourers, or hired men; and at the bottom of the social scale, bondsmen, or serfs and slaves. In the tax-exempt Persian homeland, the freeman worked for his own account. In the outlying empire, the serf was a worker attached permanently to a parcel of land, who was bought and sold with the real estate; and a slave was the property of an individual who could employ him and dispose of him at whim.

Bondsmen came from many regions and segments of society; they were war prisoners, slaves bought in foreign markets, children sold by hard-pressed parents, or freemen whose debts or crimes had reduced them to servitude. There was also a brisk and profitable trade in slave breeding. But although bondsmen and their womenfolk were not permitted to come and go at will, and were theoretically chattels of their owners, they were not necessarily destitute.

Indeed, in certain parts of the realm, notably Babylonia, servitude could even be advantageous. For instance, a Babylonian farmer, though obligated to a feudal overlord, could make a large enough profit to maintain his bondsmen in relative comfort. By contrast, the lot of a freeman in the Persian homeland could be worse than that of a slave or serf; he might earn no more than a shekel a month and could be periodically unemployed.

For that matter, certain classes of slaves—skilled workers such as builders, bakers and barbers—enjoyed even greater advantages over their free counterparts; some seem to have been allowed to draw compensation for their work, and even to go into business for themselves. Wage records kept during the construction of Persepolis indicate that slaves were compensated better than the freemen who worked alongside them.

Since slaves and serfs represented such a broad cross section of the society, their ranks naturally included intelligent and capable men. That fact, coupled with a dramatic growth in the population of slaves and serfs during the Fifth Century B.C., led to increasing competition between bondsmen and free citizens for available jobs and positions outside of manual labour. Thus, through talent and energy, slaves or serfs could attain a degree of dignity and influence; in some parts of the realm, such as Mesopotamia, they even gained the right to hold and dispose of property, including slaves of their own.

While the great estates in and around the royal capitals seem to have been managed by their fiefholders with laudable vigour and efficiency, absentee landlords created a problem in the more distant satrapies.

The difficulty, then as now, was that of keeping a man down on the farm when the pull of urban pleasures was so strong.

Though it was the practice of the Achaemenids to reward favourite Persian noblemen with valuable land grants in far-off satrapies, the recipients were often reluctant to spend much time in residence there. In fact, the system encouraged city-loving landlords to remain away from their estates for long spells, leaving superintendents in charge. As a result, what seemed a sound policy in theory was, in practice, bad both for the management of estates in particular and for the stability of the government in general.

The transportation of money and goods from distant properties to their non-resident landlords produced cash-flow problems and other managerial and financial difficulties that provided business for private banking houses, particularly in Babylonia. These firms acted also as agents and estate managers. Before the Achaemenid era, temples, and to a lesser extent royal treasuries, had performed some banking services, taking deposits and lending money. Privately owned banks—or, more accurately, wealthy merchants who handled other people's money for profit—appeared as early as the end of the Seventh Century B.C., and their importance grew with the establishment of the Persian Empire.

A clay tablet, turned up in the ruins of Nippur, records that in 537 B.C. a man named Itti-Marduk-balatu, head of a wealthy Babylonian banking family, Egibi and Sons, attended Cyrus' court at Ecbatana to conduct the kind of high-level business that has always brought banks and powerful entrepreneurs together. It is known that the Babylonian was there because, ironically and ignominiously, the wealthy banker had to borrow a pound and a half of silver from a man named Tadannu, and the tablet is the record of that petty loan contract. The banker and his associates apparently had overrun their budget for the trip and needed the cash to get home.

Such firms as Egibi and Sons lent money even to clients with doubtful credit ratings, holding as security all the income from the estate, or the slaves of an indebted owner, until the principal was repaid; the bankers had the use of the revenue and the labour while the loan remained outstanding. In this way, bankers acquired the skills of farm management, and it was a natural step thereafter to offer package deals of estate supervision to landlords who could not be bothered to administer their own farms. Firms like the Murashu bank of Nippur, whose records of the years between about 455 and 403 B.C. have informed historians of business details in Mesopotamia, would take over an estate, remitting an agreed rent to the Persian noble who owned it.

Such services demanded a many-sided organization. Besides accountants, assayers, loan officers and other money specialists, the Murashu bank's staff included horticulturalists, cattlemen, builders, transport men, brewers, experts in irrigation and dealers in agricultural produce. Murashu teams descended on neglected estates and converted them into thriving operations that yielded the bank managers annual fortunes in rents and fees, even while contributing the mandatory taxes to the royal treasury. In a typical instance described in the bank's records, Murashu's capital investments in one estate included 18 new irrigation pumps and 72 oxen to power them.

Indeed, "banking" is an inadequate word to describe the business of the House of Murashu. Its range of commercial activities rivalled in diversification those of some corporate conglomerates today. The firm would lend almost anything at a price: cash, land, dates, grain, construction materials, livestock. The organization even maintained its own stable of prostitutes, who were rented out to understaffed brothels. Murashu and similar companies were not above gouging their customers—a quarter of the harvest was their standard fee for irrigation service. Their agents acquired a reputation for underhandedness in their dealings and, at times, violence.

But for all the sharp practices—and perhaps because of them—the banks' expertise and credit facilities stood them and their customers in excellent stead until Persia's economy succumbed to an ailment often assumed to be exclusively modern: inflation, for which the banks must assume part of the blame. Among the common people, the improved standard of living that came with increased production and trade was at least partly eaten away by relentlessly rising prices. The cost of food, raw materials, manufactured products and property steadily increased during much of the life of the empire. Some scholars surmise that a noticeable decline in the number of documents regarding house sales in Babylonia over the period reflects the hard fact that houses simply became too expensive for most people to buy.

In Mesopotamia interest rates soared. Shortly before the Persian conquest of Babylonia, loan interest stood at about 20 per cent. By the end of the Fifth Century B.C. banks like Murashu were raking in 40 to 50 per cent per annum. And in Egypt conditions were as bad, if not worse.

The Persian kings, largely responsible for the empire's economic boom, must also be held accountable for much of the inflationary trouble. Blame has been placed on taxes, which over the years became more and more burdensome as the government found new ways to skim profits from the enterprises of its citizens. However, economic historians say the cause was not the rate of taxation so much as the fact that the Achaemenids hoarded state revenues, and thus shrank the money supply. Their practice of amassing wealth pulled more and more currency out of circulation and forced the public to fall back on the primitive, less fluid medium of barter. Had the treasurers put more tax revenues back into circulation in the form of coined money, business—and ultimately the empire itself—might have fared better.

It is a paradox that a shrinking money supply could have caused inflation—it is generally increased availability of money that abets inflation today. But in the more primitive economy of the Persians, scarcity of cash caused by hoarding had an opposite effect, largely by forcing up interest rates for those compelled to borrow cash to meet their obligations. People required to pay their taxes in cash had to mortgage themselves to banks to raise the money. Among the banks, the shortage of cash pushed up the price of loans, thus increasing the cost of everything else.

When the conquering Alexander of Macedonia marched into Susa in 331 B.C., he found in the Persian king's treasury 270 tons of gold coins and 1,200 tons of silver cast into ingots—a glorious trove accumulated at the expense of a once-prosperous people. Everywhere else, the Greeks encountered a populace whose loyalty to the empire was weakened by debt and resentment. Misuse of the riches that had brought the empire to unprecedented strength had contributed substantially to its demise.

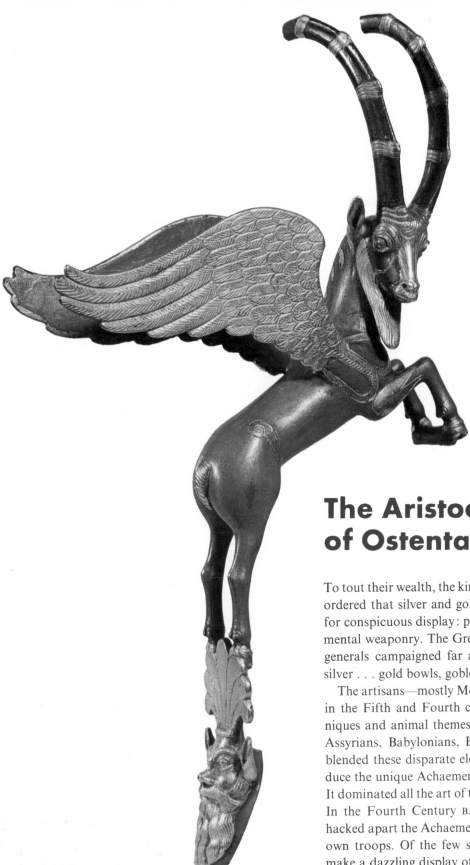

This winged ibex—a symbol for life and growth—once served as the handle of a drinking vessel. Though made in western Asia, probably for a noble, the figure, 11 inches high, shows influences from other parts of the Persian Empire. The creature's grace and vigour are typically Greek; the head it stands on represents an Egyptian demon. The gold used by Achaemenid artisans came from Bactria or Sardis, the silver from Egypt; both metals are combined in this piece.

The Aristocratic Art of Ostentation

To tout their wealth, the kings, nobles, and high-ranking soldiers of Persia ordered that silver and gold acquired by conquest be made into objects for conspicuous display: personal adornments, dining utensils and ornamental weaponry. The Greek historian Herodotus reported that Persian generals campaigned far afield accoutred with "furniture of gold and silver . . . gold bowls, goblets and drinking vessels".

The artisans—mostly Medes and Egyptians—who made these treasures in the Fifth and Fourth centuries B.C. drew freely on the artistic techniques and animal themes of many peoples who were Persian subjects: Assyrians, Babylonians, Egyptians and Ionian Greeks. The craftsmen blended these disparate elements with traditional Iranian motifs to produce the unique Achaemenid style, so named for Persia's ruling dynasty. It dominated all the art of the far-flung Persian world until the empire fell. In the Fourth Century B.C., according to one record, Greek invaders hacked apart the Achaemenid treasures to distribute the loot among their own troops. Of the few surviving pieces, the ones on these pages still make a dazzling display of opulence and technical virtuosity.

Masterworks to Satisfy Noble Vanity

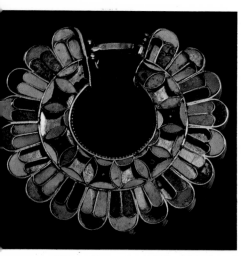

This gold ear-ring inlaid with coloured enamel was one of a pair worn by a Persian princess. Recovered from the ruins of a royal tomb at Susa, it measures almost two inches in diameter. The design was inspired by jewellery crafted in Egypt.

Two monsters—contorted lions with eagles' wings, goats' horns and horses' manes—stand poised against the five decorative discs of this five-inch-high plaque. The Persian nobleman who wore this ornament believed that the images of the fearsome beasts had the power to ward off evil. The piece was found at Hamadan, where the Greek conqueror Alexander amassed a huge hoard of Achaemenid treasures.

Griffins, once encrusted with semi-precious stones, face each other on top of an armlet that may have belonged to Cyrus or his queen. Measuring five inches across and weighing 12 ounces, it was part of a cache of treasures found near the river Oxus in an area of Afghanistan that was the Persian satrapy of Bactria. The artifacts had been deposited in a temple by worshippers seeking divine favours.

This superb gold roundel features a common Persian motif: a lion, with wings and goats' horns, half turned to snarl over its back at an imaginary pursuer. The smith who made this five-inch-wide appliqué attached 16 loops to the cord encircling the animal so the ornament could be sewn to a noble's robe. The large spaces were designed to let the garment's colour show through in handsome patterns.

Vessels for Pampered Banqueters

Two winebibbers at a banquet could pull stoppers from the spouts at the bottom of this 14-inch-high amphora and drink simultaneously. The slender ibex handles were symbolic guardians of the vessel and its contents. The use of gold and silver together is a trademark of Achaemenid artisans, who adopted the technique of mixing the metals from Egyptian craftsmen. The amphora was made in Anatolia.

This eight-inch-wide gold bowl is engraved at the rim with King Xerxes' name in Old Persian, Babylonian and Elamite—the three languages used for formal inscriptions. The script is cuneiform. Found in the trove deposited by Alexander at Hamadan, the dish may have been used to serve fruit at the banquet table of a royal Achaemenid retinue. The embossed geometric designs, similar to patterns common in Assyrian art, may be abstractions of wild berries.

The serpentine horns and ruff of a wild ram stand out sharply against the shiny surface of this seven-inch cup found at Hamadan. The long-horned ram was a symbol of Persian royal power because a dominant sheep was thought to govern its flock in the same way the King of Kings ruled the world.

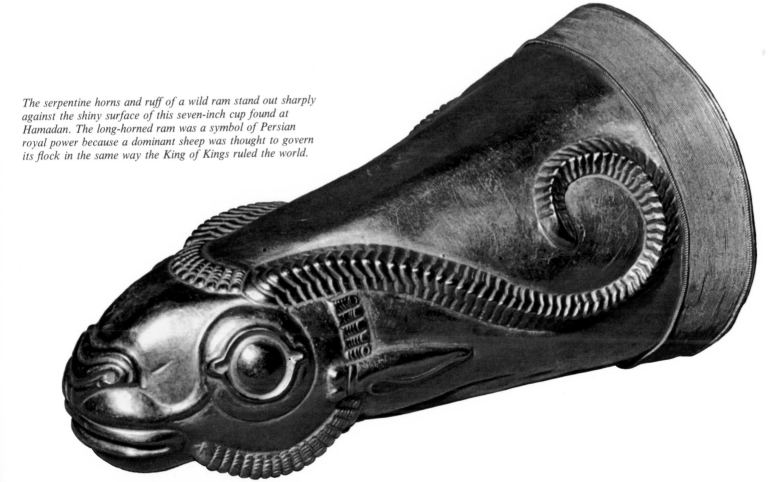

Valuable Tokens of War and the Hunt

The battle dress of a Scythian fighting man drafted into Darius' army is clearly evident in this raised gold portrait. The subject wears a peaked cap, ribbed leather body armour and a bow case hung from the waist. He brandishes a battle-axe in his left hand and a long spear in his right. The three-inch-high piece—possibly intended as an offering by a warrior to a deity before battle—is part of the Oxus Treasure found in Afghanistan.

Grimacing lions' faces and tensed claws, which form the hilt of a 17-inch-long dagger from Hamadan, were thought to impart strength to the weapon's highborn owner. Though the relatively soft gold blade is ridged for reinforcement, such weapons were usually reserved for ceremonial display; a blade meant for combat would have been made of bronze.

The scene on this gilt silver disc from the Oxus Treasure
shows how Persians outfitted themselves for hunting. They
rode on saddlecloths without stirrups and wore tunics and
trousers; their weapons were spears and arrows; their game
deer, hares and ibexes. The piece, four inches across, was
made with holes to attach it to the centre of a shield.

For the most part, the Achaemenid rulers of Persia and the aristocrats who surrounded them were realists—generators and spenders of wealth, administrators, soldiers—not poets or philosophers. In only one area did they transcend pragmatism: religion. On a spiritual plane the depth of their religious devotion places them alongside the most reverent peoples the world has ever known. Though their faith, called Zoroastrianism, was only a little older than Achaemenid sovereignty itself, it commanded the dutiful obeisance of their greatest kings.

Like Christianity and Islam, which this Persian creed foreshadowed, Zoroastrianism was at its start revolutionary. And like both of those religions, it was founded by one man, Zarathustra, better known in the Western world as Zoroaster, which is the Greek version of his name.

As conceived by him, probably shortly before 600 B.C., Zoroastrianism was an almost pure monotheism centring about a supreme being called Ahuramazda. Assisting this supreme being, as Zoroaster came to believe, was a hierarchy of subordinate spirits who were not so much divinities in their own right as different manifestations of the one true god. According to Zoroaster, Ahuramazda created man, light and darkness, and all else, both material and spiritual. Most important among the supreme deity's creations, as Zoroaster interpreted them, were two opposing forces. One, representing Truth, was called Spenta

This 36-foot tower of limestone and basalt was probably built by Darius I to house the perpetual flame, a central element in the Persians' Zoroastrian faith. Priests tended the fire, letting it burn out only when a king died; the successor rekindled the flame. Restored by excavators, this edifice stands by a cliff at Naqsh-i Rustam, located near Persepolis.

Mainyu, the Holy Spirit. The other, Angra Mainyu, the Destructive Spirit, encompassed the Lie. Both powers were constantly at work on men whose moral responsibility it was to choose between them. The great god would judge a man after death: if the man had chosen good, he would receive an eternal afterlife of ease and prosperity; if evil, his lot would be everlasting torment.

Such an organized doctrine—professing one true god and featuring ethical dualism, free will and posthumous reward and punishment—constituted a radical departure from the unsystematic polytheistic faith to which the Persians and their predecessors in Iran had long been accustomed, and to which the populace in general continued to adhere.

Possibly because Zoroaster's creed was born into a world not yet ready for it, the Persians who adopted the faith modified it into a form more compatible with older, traditional beliefs. Indeed, by the time of Achaemenid rule, some of the concepts Zoroaster had rejected as pagan or primitive had begun to reassert themselves. But some fundamental principles of Zoroastrianism were powerful enough to resist corruption and survive to influence other major faiths, especially Judaism and Christianity. Among the Jewish and Christian ideas in which scholars see a debt to Zoroastrianism is the idea of a supreme god who created not only the universe but also heaven and hell, and who on a day of judgment would mete out to the good and the wicked the eternal happiness or damnation they deserve.

The date when the Achaemenid kings first embraced Zoroastrianism is unknown. There is little evidence that it influenced Cyrus the Great or his predecessors, but there is no doubt of the devotion Darius I had for Ahuramazda, though it is uncertain whether Darius revered the god precisely according to Zoroaster's tenets. During his reign, Darius often proclaimed in royal inscriptions that he ruled by the "favour of Ahuramazda"—and significantly, no other god is mentioned. From around 480 B.C., the time of Xerxes, Darius' son and successor, there is convincing evidence that the Achaemenids had made Zoroastrianism the official Persian religion. In describing provinces he had conquered, Xerxes said: "There were places where previously the *daevas* [false gods] had been worshipped. Then by the will of Ahuramazda, I uprooted that cult of the *daevas* and I made a proclamation, 'The *daevas* shall not be worshipped!' Where the *daevas* had previously been worshipped, there did I worship Ahuramazda in accordance with the Truth and using the proper rite."

In the centuries that led up to the reign of Xerxes, the Achaemenids and their court must have experienced profound changes in moral outlook. But to understand how Zoroastrianism represented a giant step in the evolution of the Persian's religious attitudes, it is essential to look at their system of faith before the time of the Achaemenids—and to realize that many of the ancient practices, if not the beliefs, persisted in the altered framework of Zoroastrianism.

Because there are no writings that describe pre-Zoroastrian religion in ancient Iran, the scholars who attempt to reconstruct the older creeds and rites must rely on data that can only provide grounds for educated speculation. Among the sources are a few archaeological findings: principally the remains of shrines. More helpful are the scriptures of Zoroastrianism itself, the Avesta, compiled after the Persians modified the original religion and revived older beliefs, which are obliquely described. Perhaps most revealing is a much earlier non-Persian work: the Rig-Veda. Composed between 1200 and 900 B.C., it reflects the ancestral religion of the Aryan people of India, whose faith is believed to have been closely related to that of the early Iranians.

The picture that emerges from these studies reveals a polytheistic religion in which the numerous Iranian gods were divided into two classes: the *ahuras* and the *daevas*. The *ahuras* seem to have been the more lofty deities, concerning themselves mainly with the order of the universe. The two most important of these high gods probably were a deity called Ahura and another named Mithra; together they represented divine sovereignty and set the courses of the sun, moon and stars. The same gods also appear to have been associated to some extent with moral concepts: among other virtues, Mithra stood for the quality of loyalty and the sanctity of contracts; Ahura, for true speech. The gods in the second class, the *daevas*, were closer to worldly considerations, personifying such elements as earth, fire, water and winds.

Gods of both classes figured in folk myths dealing with the conflicts and hostilities men overcame, or succumbed to, in real life. But there was no all-encompassing rationale for the pantheon or for the behaviour of its members—no scheme in which men could perceive the gods' purposes or their own. The deities acted on the lives of men by whim, delivering cruelty or kindness, opposition or assistance.

Only by singing the gods' praises or by performing rituals could men hope to win divine favour. These ceremonies consisted of three basic rites, sometimes conducted in combination. One was the lighting or

maintaining of sacred fires; since the Iranians revered a fire god, they probably viewed the element he personified as a purifying agent that drove away demons.

The second ritual of the ancient religion involved the concocting of an intoxicating drink whose main ingredient was a sacred plant called *haoma*, named after a minor god of vegetation. Scholars have long puzzled over what the plant might have been and have concluded that it was a species of *Ephedra*, a medicinal herb that grows in the mountains of Iran and Afghanistan. Some of the substance was sprinkled as an offering around an altar where the invisible gods were believed to sit.

What remained of the *haoma* was saved for use in the third fundamental rite: the blood sacrifice, in which an animal, usually a bull, was slaughtered, cooked and divided among worshippers and offered to the god. *Haoma* was sprinkled over the meat before it was cooked, and the residue was mixed with milk and water, then consumed by the worshippers. The effect of the drug was to induce a state of euphoria and to impart a sense of immortality.

The figure of Zoroaster, the sage who set out to reform this deep-rooted ancient religion, stands in one of those shadows of the past that the beam of scholarship has so far failed to dispel. Historians have tried repeatedly to illuminate his life by piecing together the often apocryphal ideas of his adherents with tiny snippets of tangential information, and by speculating. Nevertheless, Zoroaster's personal story remains one of the most elusive of all time.

That, naturally, has made the man all the more intriguing. Classical writers associated Zoroaster with the Magi, a priesthood that came to control Zoroastrianism and was renowned among Greeks and Romans for their supernatural powers and their skill in sorcery. (The word "magic" is derived from their name.) They viewed Zoroaster as the supreme Magus and that image gradually eclipsed his reputation as a man of wisdom.

Some of the misconceptions surrounding Zoroaster were pierced in the 18th Century A.D. when the Avesta—the holy book written in an Iranian dialect akin to Sanskrit and long unknown to the Western world—was finally translated by the French Orientalist Abraham Hyacinthe Anquetil-Dupperon. Zoroastrian tradition says that the Avesta was originally inscribed during the prophet's lifetime in gold ink on 12,000 oxhides and later deposited in a royal library near Persepolis, where it was destroyed when Alexander the Great burned the Achaemenid capital in 330 B.C. Actually, the Avesta was compiled as a body of oral traditions over many centuries, and probably was inscribed for the first time in the Third and Fourth centuries A.D. Though only a third of the original text survives, Anquetil-Dupperon's translation was instrumental in revealing Zoroaster as prophet and religious reformer behind the wizard's façade.

But he remained disconcertingly ill-defined. Even today scholars can only conjecture about the details of his personal history. However, they have managed to glimpse an outline of his life that seems to bear some resemblance to truth by separating what appear to be the factual from the fantastic accounts in the Avesta and from those in a corpus of religious works by Zoroastrian clerics of the Ninth Century A.D. (The latter especially, known as the Pahlavi books, are heavily laced with miracles and other wondrous happenings.)

These books suggest that Zoroaster first came to prominence 258 years before Alexander—meaning before Alexander's razing of Persepolis in 330 B.C. This date, 588 B.C., is taken to indicate the year he made his first important convert, King Vishtaspa, whose realm was in eastern Iran. Vishtaspa's conversion is said to have occurred when Zoroaster was 40 years old, dating the prophet's birth at 628 B.C.

Tradition locates Zoroaster's birthplace in northwestern Iran, in what is now a suburb of the modern city of Tehran. As a youth Zoroaster may have served as a Magus, or priest, in the old polytheistic religion. But at the age of 20 he set out to find enlightenment, which came 10 years later in the form of a vision of the god Ahuramazda, who taught Zoroaster the principles of his faith. Driven from his homeland when he proclaimed his unorthodox views, Zoroaster wandered for a decade, preaching his message but making few converts. Realizing that he needed a power base for his religion, he sought out Vishtaspa and after two years finally succeeded in winning him over.

Vishtaspa's entire court was soon converted, and Zoroastrianism spread widely through eastern Iran. But even with a royal champion, the triumph of the new faith apparently was far from peaceful. At Zoroaster's urging, King Vishtaspa's army eventually launched a belligerent campaign to win converts by force. Priests and princes of older beliefs could naturally have been expected to try blocking the spread of the prophet's message, and one reasonable version of Zoroaster's death relates that he was killed during a religious war at the age of 77.

Scholars have not had an easy time determining precisely what the prophet's original teachings were.

This Eighth Century B.C. *structure—viewed here from above—housed a cult dedicated to fire, which was traditionally revered in Iran. In 1965, near the Median city of Ecbatana, archaeologists discovered the temple filled with shale and capped with bricks —possibly an act of deconsecration at the death of a sovereign. Removing the debris revealed the yard-high altar in the foreground and the decorative niches four feet tall that were hewn in the walls.*

The answers must lie within the Avesta itself, and specifically in a group of hymns called the Gathas, which Zoroaster is thought to have composed. But the sage's own phrases were probably never written down; the texts that Anquetil-Dupperon and subsequent experts used for translation were finally recorded nearly a thousand years after the prophet lived and preached. During that interval the prayers quite certainly underwent little change. But when they were at last committed to writing, around the Fourth Century A.D., it was in a language, called Avestan, that still defies complete comprehension. What Anquetil-Dupperon pored over for a full decade continues to confound scholars. The meaning of individual words is still in dispute—giving rise to disagreement about entire concepts.

Interpretations range from the idea that Zoroaster's teaching departed little from the accepted practice that preceded him to the radical view that his ideas made a total break with Iran's religious past. The latter extreme theory prevails today among students of Zoroastrian theology.

According to this school of thought, Zoroaster selected from the old pantheon one supreme god, Ahura—also called Ahuramazda—by sweeping aside all the other *ahuras*. (The cognate "mazda", a Persian word for "wise", was already part of the deity's name before Zoroaster's time.)

In addition to the qualities of good and evil, Zoroaster attributed to Ahuramazda the origin of all matter. The lesser deities, the *daevas*, he reduced to mere demons. Just below Ahuramazda, Zoroaster placed a holy spirit through whom the supreme god expressed his will. He also endowed Ahuramazda with six assistants called the Amesha Spentas—Bounte-

ous Immortals—who stood for Truth and all other virtues; they were presented as aspects of the one true god and as qualities attainable by men.

Though the idea that good and evil are antagonistic was not original with Zoroaster—the concept was present in the earlier Iranian religion—he made the struggle universal, describing it in his creed as a clash between Ahuramazda's Spenta Mainyu, the Holy Spirit, and the wicked Angra Mainyu.

This conflict was crucial to Zoroaster's faith. While man was free to follow the moral principle of his choice, Zoroaster cautioned him to decide with a clear mind, since the hereafter Ahuramazda would reward the evil with long torment and the righteous with bliss. Thus Zoroaster's god worked according to a system; unlike the old gods who had dealt with man at whim, Ahuramazda stated the rules in advance.

For all Zoroaster's contributions to religious cohesiveness, his new theology relied heavily on traditional rituals. He viewed fire as the most sacrosanct element, a gift of Ahuramazda to man and a symbol of truth because of its power to dispel darkness—the realm of Angra Mainyu. He therefore made fire the primary instrument of worship. Bull sacrifices remained an important part of the rites, though the prophet objected to the customary cruel method of cutting the throat of the fully conscious animal.

Another example of Zoroaster's moderating temperament lay in his attitude towards the use of *haoma*. He may have banned its use altogether; some scholars, though, think he only proscribed the excessive and orgiastic use of the drug. If he did ban the ritual, the reform was short-lived. There is evidence in parts of the Avesta that the drinking of *haoma* was a central feature of Zoroastrian worship.

In such fashion the basic beliefs and rituals of Zoroaster's religion can be outlined, but its evolution is more difficult to trace. How the creed was carried to the Persians, and when and why it underwent changes after its adoption by the Achaemenid kings, are questions not susceptible to hard answers.

Certainly by the time of Xerxes' successor, Artaxerxes I, Zoroastrianism was no longer the unalloyed faith preached by Zoroaster. By about 441 B.C. the monotheistic core of the religion had quite certainly atrophied. In that year, Artaxerxes reorganized the Persian calendar and in doing so named the months for older gods who had been purged by Zoroaster. King Artaxerxes II testified to the extent of the corruption when he ordered inscribed on his palace at Susa this prayer: "May Ahuramazda, Anahita [whose name came to be associated with the Babylonian mother-goddess Ishtar and with the Greek Artemis], and Mithra protect me from all evil." In his statement Artaxerxes was clearly equating, or nearly so, Ahuramazda with gods who had no real connection with Zoroaster's vision.

Of all the ancient Iranian gods who became prominent in the emerging hybrid religion, Mithra was the most significant. Formerly regarded mainly as the guardian of contractual sanctity, Mithra became almost as important as Ahuramazda himself in a new multiple role: god of the light that precedes the dawn, protector of all Iranians and great war deity. As god of combat, Mithra assumed some of the terrible traits of an ancient war spirit, a wrathful, mace-wielding *daeva* known in the Rig-Veda as Indra.

Many scholars attribute to the Magi the gradual erosion of pure Zoroastrianism. As members of a hereditary priesthood, the Magi had for centuries worked as religious functionaries in whatever Iranian faith happened to be dominant at a given time. Thus it was logical that they should administer Zoroastrianism when it became the Achaemenid faith. But they acted in the service of what must have been a fundamentally conservative laity; the Persian nobility presumably was not inclined to supplant all customary beliefs with radical new tenets. To consolidate their position as professionals, therefore, the Magi may have been responsible for the actual fusing of old forms of worship with the new ones that Zoroastrianism demanded. Furthermore, as political realists, the Achaemenid rulers would have avoided alienating their subjects in the interest of a rigid dogma; religious tolerance was a virtue for which the Achaemenids became renowned. Though many of the Great Kings professed themselves to be worshippers of Ahuramazda, they did not insist that their subjects take the same course.

Nevertheless, the Magi's precise role in the evolution of Zoroastrianism is unclear. To writers in Classical Greece and Rome the Magi were notorious as magicians and astrologers, and followed such unseemly practices as incest. They did not bury their dead, exposing the corpses instead to be devoured by vultures and wild beasts. Herodotus was also appalled by their alleged cruelty. The Magi, he wrote, "not only kill anything, except dogs and men, with their own hands, but make a special point of doing so; ants, snakes, animals, birds—no matter what they kill, they kill them indiscriminately."

Herodotus, however, may have judged the Magi in ignorance. What he saw as wanton cruelty could have been a Magian belief that many creatures represented evil powers and therefore deserved killing. And the exposure of the dead that horrified Classical writers seems to have stemmed from the Zoroastrian idea that the earth, like fire, was sacred; to bury or cremate the dead would have defiled these elements.

Even though Herodotus and other Classical writers recorded many details about the Magi of Achaemenid

*The ruins of two limestone altars, about seven feet high, stand
solitary in a section of Pasargadae. Both were erected by
Cyrus II around 545 B.C. Scholars speculate that the monarch
ascended the stepped altar (foreground) and in an attitude of
devotion faced the other structure, which held a sacred fire.
Confirming this theory are royal tomb carvings at Naqsh-i
Rustam (page 104), which represent the sovereign and a
sacrosanct flame on similarly opposed platforms.*

times, little is known about how Zoroastrian adherents of that period performed their rituals of worship. Reliefs on Darius' tomb and those of his successors show kings worshipping before a holy fire while a winged disc symbolizing Ahuramazda floats overhead. As in pre-Zoroastrian days, such fires were kindled and maintained in special buildings usually constructed as towers.

The remains of five tower temples from the Achaemenid period have been found. The most famous is the structure that stands in front of the tomb of Darius the Great at Naqsh-i Rustam (*page 92*). Far more elaborate was a tower whose ruins were unearthed in the 1960s at Dahan-i Ghulaman, a site close to the border of Afghanistan and Iran.

Constructed sometime between 600 and 400 B.C. and made entirely of mud brick—stone was scarce in the region—it was an enormous, nearly square building, each of its outer walls measuring about 175 feet. Inside was a large court, at the centre of which stood three altars hollowed to hold sacred flames. Excavators of the site believe the altars were dedicated to the same triad of deities addressed by King Artaxerxes II in his palace inscription: Ahuramazda, Anahita and Mithra. In porticoes along the interior walls were fire ovens; near by were pits containing bone fragments, evidence that animal sacrifice was part of the rituals conducted in the building.

Strabo, the Greek geographer of the First Century B.C., set down a description of such a fire temple in use. Although he lived almost 300 years after the end of the Achaemenid Dynasty, it is believed that he based his account on the eyewitness reports of Greek historians who accompanied Alexander the Great on his Persian campaign and whose observations were preserved by succeeding generations. It seems likely, therefore, that the ritual Strabo described can be traced to Achaemenid times.

"The Persians," Strabo wrote, "have . . . certain large shrines called Pyraetheia [places where fire is kindled]. In the middle of these is an altar, on which is a great quantity of ashes, where the Magi maintain an unextinguished fire. They enter daily and continue their incantation for nearly an hour, holding before the fire a bundle of rods, and wear round their heads high turbans of felt, reaching down . . . to cover the lips and the sides of the cheeks." The Greek also commented that such worshippers "do not blow the flame with their breath, but fan it; those who have blown on the flame . . . or thrown any dead thing or dirt upon the fire are put to death". It seems logical to assume that the priests wore mouth coverings to avoid the risk that their own breath would contaminate the fire. Strabo did not say whether worshippers other than priests took part in this daily service.

No description exists of a *haoma* ceremony of the Achaemenid period, although this rite must have been performed regularly. But from hints in the Avesta and from Zoroastrian practices of later times, it is possible to form a reasonable idea of how a *haoma* ritual was conducted in ancient Persia.

The ceremony took place in a fire temple and centred about the sacred flames. It was conducted twice—once for the priests only and immediately thereafter for the holy men and laity together. The rite lasted from dawn to dusk, and once it was underway, the priests could not stop to rest, eat or even relieve themselves. One of their first acts was the slaying of a bull, probably by stunning it mercifully with a club before cutting its throat. It was believed that the

Living Celebrants of a Venerable Creed

The Parsees of India are modern Zoroastrians, direct descendants of Persians who left their homeland in the Eighth Century A.D. rather than accept the religion of their Muslim conquerors. Though they have a few counterparts still in Iran—their ancestors went underground rather than flee—most Parsees live in Bombay, where they have become prosperous business and community leaders, having adopted the Hindu language and Indian or western dress and customs.

But they remain adamantly faithful to the rites of their ancient belief, among which are a joyous celebration of the new year, the maintenance of a perpetual flame attended by veiled priests, the use of the sacred liquor called *haoma* as a ceremonial offering and the ritual investing of neophytes with a tunic and girdle that signify full-fledged membership in the faith. Parsees do not accept converts or permit marriage with people of other faiths, which helps account for their dwindling number; there are only 85,000 left—a drop of 31,000 since 1951.

A seven-year-old Parsee is initiated as a Zoroastrian at a Navjote ceremony in Bombay; a priest invests the boy with the sudra and kusti—the sacred shirt and belt that orthodox members of the faith have worn ever since the time of the prophet.

At a Jashan, a ceremony commemorating the completion of
a fire temple in Bombay, an elder Parsee priest—one of a
group witnessing the rite—ladles fragrant sandalwood on to
the holy fire. As in ancient Persia, the celebrant wears a veil
to prevent his breath from contaminating the flame.

slaughter symbolically anticipated an event that was to occur at the end of time, when the ultimate sacrificial bull would be slain by a saviour.

Following the bull sacrifice, the priests prepared the *haoma* to be consumed during the ritual. Carvings on gem seals found in the ruins of Persepolis depict one priest carrying three rod-shaped objects that presumably were twigs of the *haoma* plant. On a table beside the fire altar stands the pestle and mortar in which another priest has crushed the plant to symbolize the self-sacrifice of the plant god, Haoma.

The juice thus produced was mixed with the flesh of the bull and, after reciting hymns in praise of Ahuramazda, the priests consumed a special *haoma* that rendered all good men physically and spiritually immortal. Savouring a drug-induced taste of the true immortality that awaited them in the hereafter, the congregation spent the remainder of the day listening to the priests recite in their entirety the Gathas and other hymns venerating the Bounteous Immortals, the sacred fire and the older gods who had become re-established as Zoroastrian deities.

Zoroastrianism outlasted the Achaemenids. Although dormant for about five centuries after Alexander's conquest, the religion was revived as the official Persian creed by another line of kings, the Sasanian Dynasty (*pages 147-153*), which lasted from the Third Century A.D. until the Muslims overran Iran in 642. During that period it once again approached the monotheism preached by Zoroaster; the gods who had come to share divine honours with Ahuramazda faded into the background.

The religion is still practised today by some 10,000 tenacious believers in Iran and by about 100,000 in India—descendants of Zoroastrians, known as Parsees after their native Persia, who fled in the Eighth Century A.D. to escape the rule of Islam.

But Zoroaster's legacy is not confined to his few surviving followers in India and the Middle East. His ideas, although some were altered or contaminated, were given a tremendous impetus westwards by the Achaemenid kings. While the monarchs did not try to force Zoroastrianism on subject countries, the fact that the imperial rulers adopted the religion enabled

A 16-foot-high carving on the tomb of Artaxerxes III near Persepolis establishes the king as a worshipper of the Zoroastrian god, Ahuramazda. The monarch stands on a three-tiered platform opposite a fire altar similarly elevated. The sacred blaze and Artaxerxes' raised hand are parts of a ritual confirming reverence for the deity, whose winged image hovers overhead. The moon over the altar may be a divinity associated with Ahuramazda: Mithra, the god of light.

the prophet's thoughts to reach peoples who might otherwise have been untouched by the faith.

Thus some of Zoroaster's ideas found their way into the religion of the ancient Israelites, an influence that is relatively easy to trace because of the Jews' exile in Babylon. They had been dragged away from Jerusalem with one set of religious concepts; but after Babylon fell to Cyrus the Great and became part of the expanding Persian Empire, they were sent home—inevitably with new perspectives drawn from their Babylonian experience.

Before the period of bondage, Jews believed that all souls of the dead—good and bad alike—were consigned to Sheol, an underworld clothed in thick darkness. It was only after their contact with the Persians that an afterlife offering reward or punishment entered their reckoning. Significantly, the first of the Biblical authors to express this new belief was Daniel, who served as an official in the administration of King Darius. "Many of those who sleep in the dust of the earth will awake," he said, "some to everlasting life and some to the reproach of eternal abhorrence." Later the Jewish sect that gave strongest support to this doctrine was that of the Pharisees, whose name, according to some, meant Persians.

It could be said that Zoroaster also gave Judaism its concept of the devil. In Biblical scriptures dealing with times prior to the Babylonian exile, Satan was an agent of the Almighty, obeying his master's orders. He had to request the Lord's permission, for example, before tormenting Job. After the Jews were exposed to the concept of Angra Mainyu—Zoroastrianism's embodiment of evil—Satan became a powerful figure counterposed to God.

The Dead Sea Scrolls—written in the Second or First Century B.C. by members of a Jewish sect and discovered in 1947 in a cave on the northwest coast of the sea—may also reflect Zoroaster's effect on Judaism. One of the texts, the *Manual of Discipline*, which was originally written just after the Babylonian exile ended, says that God made for man two spirits: "They are the spirits of truth and error. In the abode of light are the origins of truth, and from the source of darkness are the origins of error. . . . One of the spirits God loves for all ages of eternity, and with all its deeds he is pleased for ever; as for the other, he abhors its company, all its ways he hates for ever." According to parts of the Avesta apparently composed by Zoroaster some time during the Seventh Century B.C., this is precisely the way the god Ahuramazda felt about his own creations: Spenta Mainyu and Angra Mainyu.

Christians, in turn, are heirs not only to the Zoroastrian concepts that lodged in Judaism—but also, possibly, to others. In the Book of Revelations, the disciple John sends to his fellow Christians peace from God "and from the seven spirits who are before his throne". These attendants of God, the archangels, may have been derived from Spenta Mainyu and the six Bounteous Immortals around Ahuramazda.

Perhaps Zoroastrianism ultimately withered to near-insignificance among the world's religions because it was never widely embraced by the Persian populace at large. Even after its revival as the official Persian creed in Sasanian times, its adherents were still mainly members of the ruling class. In some ways, the fate of Zoroastrianism can be likened to that of the palaces of the Achaemenid kings at Persepolis. Alexander the Great destroyed the royal dwellings but spared the homes of the humble.

Sacked and burned by Alexander the Great's conquering army, shaken by uncounted earthquakes, eroded by 20 centuries of rain, rock-breaking temperatures and scouring winds, looted by men who sought treasure, Persepolis—the greatest of the five royal residences of Persia—is a definitive ancient ruin.

Yet the place remains an awesomely impressive sight 2,500 years after it was built. Even in decay Persepolis dominates the southwestern Iranian plain on which it lies. Built as a citadel on top of a broad, natural rock platform or terrace, the site rises 40 to 50 feet above its surroundings. The giant columns of the Achaemenids' palaces and treasure houses no longer bear the weight of roof beams, but more than a dozen pillars—slender and elegant—still stand. The fortified mud-brick walls that once almost totally enclosed the buildings on the terrace have long since worn away, but colossal stone bulls still guard the citadel's main gate. Now faceless, these ancient sentries continue to intimidate visitors who climb the broad stairs to the terrace on which the ruins stand. And within the gate, carved images of the men who once crowded the huge palaces and vast columnar halls—powerful kings, crown princes, Persian nobles, dignitaries of subject countries, stalwart soldiers—are still there, maintaining silent occupancy, their forms cut into the stone faces of monumental staircases and doorways.

Darius I and his Achaemenid successors called

This majestic visage of polished black limestone—nearly 20 inches from brow to chin—once stared down from the capital of a 33-foot column in a council hall at the ceremonial city of Persepolis. Similar faces, representing guardian spirits, met visitors at the city's main gate and loomed over royal personages passing through many of the great buildings.

their most ambitious of residences Parsa, the name by which the surrounding province, the Persian homeland, was also known. The Greeks, however, called the city Perseptolis, meaning "destroyer of cities", in bitter tribute to the destruction that had been wrought by Persia in Greece; from that name has come Persepolis, a corruption of the Greek by which the citadel has commonly, though incorrectly, been known ever since.

When the Achaemenids chose the site some time before 520 B.C., they sought a place far apart from their everyday concerns. In their thinking, they gave no consideration to convenience or habitability—there was not even an easily accessible source of water. And while Persepolis was only 45 miles from Pasargadae, the coronation city, it was more than 300 miles from the empire's administrative capital, Susa, where the Achaemenids necessarily spent most of their time. Not really a city, not primarily a fortress, Persepolis was a gigantic living monument—a conspicuous demonstration of the Persians' rise from rude nomads to world masters, a colossally immodest salute to their own glory.

The very difficulties inherent in Persepolis' environment seem to have struck the Persians as assets. For one thing, its remoteness ensured the exclusivity of state rituals performed there and provided a measure of safety for the hoard of treasure kept in the citadel. Moreover, the distance of the site from other human habitation called attention to the special nature of the kings' status above and apart from their subjects, and made the place appropriate not only for celebrations but also for royal burials. (The tombs of four Achaemenid kings, including Darius and Xerxes, are cut into the face of Naqsh-i Rustam, the site of a

Persepolis' ruins had already drawn European travellers for more than two centuries when this engraving was published in 1725. The French artist included a compatriot with two turbaned guides (far left) admiring the wreckage of the throne hall (centre, foreground), once decorated with a hundred interior pillars.

massive rock outcropping four miles north of Persepolis [*pages 138-139*]; three other kings were given impressive burials at sites close to the capital.) Finally, Persepolis' natural rock platform, which rises abruptly above the plain on three sides and backs into the slope of a low mountain on the fourth, was easy to defend.

The scheme for this unique metropolis unfolded over 60 years of construction. To start, the Persian builders strengthened the sides of the citadel's natural foundation, the terrace, with a retaining wall of gargantuan limestone blocks, flattened some areas of the surface and filled in others to produce three graded building levels, and cut a system of large subsurface drainage conduits into the bedrock. They then pulled together talent, skill, materials and inspiration from throughout their empire, taking ideas as well as craftsmen from their subject provinces, and used them all to create one of the most magnificent assemblages of buildings ever seen.

Although the ancient grandeur of Persepolis has been legendary ever since the Greeks brought it to ruin, it was not until the early 1930s, when archaeologists first began scientific excavation of the site,

that anyone was able to reclaim any sense of its original splendour or of its builders' ingenuity.

Before then, of course, many travellers had marvelled at what they could see of the city's remains. In 1619 a European visitor had counted 20 standing columns, which once supported the roof of Persepolis' most imposing building: a great edifice that archaeologists now call the apadana, or audience hall.

By 1841 only 13 columns of the apadana remained erect, the same number standing today. After the Islamic conquest of Iran in the Seventh Century A.D., generation after generation of Muslims, motivated by religious abhorrence of art embodying human figures, defaced the exposed reliefs that covered the building walls in order to obliterate the carved stone faces pictured on them. Other defacements were more frivolous. As early as 1818 a visitor wrote of his examination of Persepolis' gateway: "I am sorry to say, I found a cloud of initials, and names, and dates, of former visitants to the site, to the no small injury of the fine surface of the stone." Such destruction, abetted by the ravages of the climate, had long since stripped off all but a few specks of the paint that had once gaily decorated the walls and carvings.

The first systematic digging at Persepolis began in 1931. The work was mounted by the University of Chicago's Oriental Institute, but its first director was an archaeologist from the University of Berlin, Ernst Herzfeld, who had been studying the ruins independently for several years. Now with the support of the large American team, Herzfeld found riches that had been concealed from treasure seekers for more than 20 centuries. After the debris had been cleared from the floor of the apadana, an architect with the expedition, Friedrich Krefter, noticed a square hole cut in the northwest corner of the rock floor. He deduced that the Persians, who loved symmetry, might have sunk similar holes at the remaining three corners of the floor. He was correct. Workers found three more holes, two of which still contained stone boxes 18 inches square and six inches high. Inside each of the boxes were one gold and one silver plaque. All four of the precious documents bore identical messages inscribed in three languages—Old Persian, Elamite and Babylonian—that "Darius the Great King, King of Kings" addressed to posterity: "This is the kingdom I hold, from the Scythians who are beyond Sogdiana, thence unto Kush; from India, thence unto Sardis, which Ahuramazda the greatest of the gods bestowed upon me."

Herzfeld's second season of excavation brought additional thrilling discoveries. Probably the most interesting feature of the visible ruins was the enormous relief of a ceremonial tribute procession that extends for more than 260 feet along the walls of a double staircase at the north end of the apadana. Unfortunately, exposed as it was, the relief had suffered the worst of the ravages of man and nature. Pieces were missing, figures were battered beyond recognition and centuries of erosion had blurred the details. Consequently, there was more than a little interest within the camp when workmen digging on the apadana's east side laid bare the top of what appeared to be a second sculpture-ornamented staircase.

As the rubble and dust that had once been the apadana's 17-foot-thick mud-brick wall were carefully removed from the stairway on to which the structure had collapsed, carvings slowly came into view. Excitement increased as it was realized that the relief was a mirror image of the same scene shown on the northern staircase, but in excellent condition. Vast in size, severe in its ornamental style, it has not only provided an invaluable record of the best of Achaemenid art, but has also captured for posterity the distinctive costume and physical appearances of 23 ancient peoples (*pages 35-43*).

Herzfeld's successes continued. In a building archaeologists have named the throne hall he unearthed another foundation record: "Artaxerxes the king speaks," it read in Babylonian. "This house Xerxes the king, my father, laid its foundations . . . I, Artaxerxes the king, built and brought [it] to completion." The history of Persepolis' construction was steadily being pieced together.

But despite his contributions to the body of knowledge of Persepolis, Herzfeld's brilliant reputation was marred by the unsystematic way in which he published his finds. He presented several papers on Persepolis, but they lacked the sort of meticulous technical data that younger generations of archaeologists find so essential. In vain they looked in Herzfeld's reports for precise descriptions of how and where he had found his artifacts, what their condition had been and what other materials had been discovered near them.

After three years as field director of the Persepolis expedition, Herzfeld resigned. His replacement was an experienced archaeologist from the University of Chicago, Erich Schmidt. Schmidt's approach to the work at Persepolis was more organized than Herzfeld's. He went to great pains to supply the documentation omitted by his predecessor. His own investigations of Persepolis were reported in three enormous, comprehensive volumes. Schmidt meticulously noted where he had found almost every fragment of clay tablet, arrowhead and nail. And he enlisted specialists to analyse the composition of plasters, asphalt and glass, and also to determine exactly how they had been made.

Among the major finds credited to Schmidt's efforts were seven limestone foundation tablets bearing important texts, one of them Xerxes' proscription of pre-Zoroastrian religious beliefs. Schmidt also uncovered a multi-roomed complex identified as the treasury. It no longer contained much in the way of precious metals—Alexander had removed most of them—but it did yield some finds of greater value to archaeologists and historians: royal domestic utensils, weapons, a cache of 753 clay tablets inscribed in Elamite and a stunning pair of large stone reliefs (*pages 48-49*), which represent a king, attended by his retinue, giving audience.

The discovery of the Elamite tablets caused tremendous excitement among scholars. Immediately one of Schmidt's colleagues from Chicago, a philologist named George Cameron, began the difficult task of translation. Though Elamite continued to be spoken until about A.D. 1000, it remained a poorly understood language—"almost a *lingua incognita*," Cameron said. It took him several years to unlock the treasury tablets' secrets, and what he found was not the hoped-for history of the empire but financial documents on receipts and disbursements between 492 and 459 B.C. Cameron's tablets were, however, very valuable in unveiling the history of the city's construction: where workers came from, how much they were paid and when projects waxed and waned.

Through the tablets and inscriptions found at Persepolis, it is known that Darius ordered the start of Persepolis' construction about 520 B.C. His labourers prepared the terrace, constructed the monumental staircase that leads up to it, built the portal and much of the treasury, constructed a palace and started the apadana. His son Xerxes set about finishing the apadana and building the great bull-guarded Gate of All Lands. Xerxes also commissioned another palace, a structure that Herzfeld thought was a harem, and began the throne hall. Xerxes' successor, Artaxerxes I, arranged for completion of the throne hall and the start of work on a second grand gateway that was never finished. Building ceased about the middle of the Fifth Century B.C. at which time the empire shuddered under a succession of weak and corrupt rulers. A full century passed before Artaxerxes III resumed construction—and 25 years later Persepolis was burned to the ground.

The motives and purposes of the kings who built Persepolis come to life in the thousands of linear feet of carved stone reliefs found throughout the ruins. From study of these scenes, scholars have concluded that Persepolis was primarily intended for ceremonial use during the New Year's festivities. However, there remain countless unanswered questions and contradictory theories about Persepolis and just what went on there.

Was the building Herzfeld called a harem actually such, or was it a series of supplemental storerooms for the treasury next door, as some scholars now think? Did Darius and Xerxes ever in fact reside in the palaces that bear their names, or were these buildings used exclusively for public entertaining?

The latter possibility was reinforced in 1952 by the discovery of ruins on a site removed from the main buildings, down on the plain. These remains were identified by an inscription as a palace of Xerxes, and thus indicated that the king might have had his residence not in the heart of Persepolis but in a separate dwelling. If so, the circumstance would also answer the harem question; if the king himself lived on the plain, it is not likely that he kept his wives and concubines in the upper city.

In considering other buildings, some archaeologists assert that the throne hall was not an audience chamber at all but a royal museum where riches were displayed. One theorist has suggested that the edifice was a kind of hall of honour for the army—a theory based largely on the evidence of a relief there that shows soldiers supporting the throne.

Despite such uncertainties, enough is now known —or can be surmised—about Persepolis to help the modern student visualize what the place was like when it was alive and growing. The story of the city's construction is chronicled in numerous inscriptions and tablets, which provide not only the nationalities of workers, but also the names of Persian officials. The comments of Classical authors also help form a picture of life at the Achaemenids' courts. The Greek Xenophon never saw Persepolis, but he spent years in military service under the Persians and wrote in detail about their customs. Ctesias, another Greek, wrote memoirs on his 20 years as physician to Artaxerxes I. And the Biblical Book of Esther describes life at the court of Susa.

Thus it is possible, by drawing on all these sources and, where they differ, by accepting those that most appeal to common sense, to sketch an image of the Achaemenid capital as it might actually have been seen by some visitor from a distant town—and to get a pretty good idea of the visitor as well.

The time is early in the month of Viyaxna (March) in the year 467 B.C., dated in the Persian calendar as

the 19th year of Xerxes' reign. Down the western approach road to Parsa comes the young Elamite Bakabaadda, mounted on a donkey; he is about to begin a new job in a new city. Bakabaadda should be exhausted after the longest journey of his life; he has travelled more than 300 miles from his home town of Susa, but he is much too excited to be tired. At last he is in Parsa.

Bakabaadda is a scribe, as were his father and grandfather before him. In scribal school he learned to read and write in four languages: Persian, Aramaic, Babylonian and his own tongue, Elamite. And he mastered arithmetic, which is the reason the chancellery in Susa chose to send him when the treasurer of Parsa issued a call for clerical help. After more than a decade of inactivity while Great King Xerxes fought the Greeks, construction at Parsa is again proceeding at a feverish pace. Now there are more than 1,300 workmen to be paid and provisioned, and records on daily shipments of building materials must be maintained. Bakabaadda's facility with numbers will be very useful.

A hint of morning is in the sky, but the shadow of the mountain the young man is approaching lets him

This five-foot detail of a lion and bull in combat is a recurrent theme among Persepolis' sculptures. Its meaning challenges scholars. Some think the scene represents seasonal change at the time of the vernal equinox: the lion, symbol of the summer sun, defeats the bull, winter's rain. Other experts note that at Persepolis, come dusk on the equinox, the constellation Leo (the lion) is at its zenith and Taurus (the bull) is setting.

see only a vague outline of the great walled terrace at its base. Near by, sounds of movement and voices begin to issue from the sprawl of mud-brick huts that line the road. Labourers and servants are rousing themselves for the day. There is now sufficient light to see that behind the workers' houses are high walls over which the tops of trees are visible. From his grandfather's descriptions, Bakabaadda knows that these walls away from the road enclose the landscaped gardens and stately homes of the wealthy.

As he passes the entrance of one of these estates, the gate suddenly flies open and two boys dash out, causing Bakabaadda's donkey to shy. Each boy carries a drinking cup in one hand and a chunk of bread in the other; they head at a run in the direction of the school within the citadel. Bakabaadda is not impressed by what he knows of the curriculum: no tablet and stylus to master, no words or numbers to learn. These boys spend most of their time practising marksmanship with arrows and spears, and studying Persian law.

And when their schooling is over, will they then start enjoying life? Not Persians, Bakabaadda thinks. No, they will spend the next 10 years hunting with the king by day and spending every night on guard duty outside the city's public buildings, sleeping in relays on the ground. Even if they were to get married during that time, they would nonetheless be expected to appear frequently for the night watch.

The scribe nudges his mount along a path that angles off towards the southern extremity of the citadel on the terrace. At last he reaches open ground near the southwest corner of Parsa. He stops and stares. Proud as he is of his native city, he is impressed. Susa, too, has a palace complex on a raised

terrace, but nothing on this scale. The long front of the terrace, a forbidding rampart of limestone 45 feet high, stretches a quarter of a mile to the north. On top of the rampart rises another wall, this one of mud brick, 40 feet high and 30 feet wide. It reaches in parallel rows from the base of the mountain in the background and partially encircles the buildings at the front of the terrace. Most of the front of the terrace stands so high above the plain that it needs no fortification wall.

Even from his low vantage Bakabaadda has an unobstructed view of the great apadana poised on the lip of the platform. The flat-roofed structure is an awesome 300 feet wide. The 14 black limestone columns of its western portico are seven feet in diameter and yet soar so high—65 feet—that they look almost weightless. Bakabaadda notices that the stout wall guarding the sides of the terrace is reinforced at intervals by high, bulky battle towers that measure 60 feet square. A similar line of fortifications climbs to the crest of the mountain.

But time is precious; he must not stand here gaping all day. He boots his donkey and hastens to obtain lodging and report to his new employer.

At the foot of the terrace Bakabaadda finds an inn. Since the New Year's festivities are less than a month away, the landlord is reluctant to give permanent space to a scribe when he can fill his beds with the big spenders from Babylon or Memphis who will be arriving soon. But he yields when Bakabaadda mentions that he will be employed by Vahush, the treasurer of Parsa.

Bed and board thus arranged, the young Elamite leaves his donkey in the inn stable and goes off to

A Setting for Rare and Princely Feasts

For his personal use when celebrating the new year at Persepolis, King Darius ordered the construction of the palatial building whose ruins appear at right. Here, the sovereign and his son Xerxes held feasts and prepared themselves to hold court in the adjacent apadana, or main audience hall.

Though called Darius' palace, the edifice was not equipped as a residence; its decorations suggest more limited purposes. Reliefs on the doorjambs of two outer rooms show attendants with towels and bottles of cosmetics, indicating that the king and crown prince used the chambers to wash and dress. Other carvings show servants bringing food for the royal table. Xerxes later built an even grander banquet hall for himself.

In this view from the south, windows and door frames dominate the ruins of the 50-foot-square dining hall where Darius and Xerxes feasted. Reliefs of guards fighting animals, and servants are carved on the façade of the stairway. Four sculptured columns of the apadana rise in the background.

check in for work. He walks through long rows of pine trees planted in front of the terrace and finds himself before a huge double staircase. Steps more than 20 feet in width rise left and right to landings about halfway up and then turn inwards, the two upper flights converging on a central landing at the top. The steps have treads a foot deep and risers only four inches or so high; Bakabaadda ascends almost without being aware of climbing. He is just thinking how easily a horse could negotiate such a staircase when two mounted soldiers clatter by on their way up.

At the top he is confronted by a pair of colossal winged bulls carved in relief on either side of the west doorway of the gatehouse, which appears to be about 40 feet high. The giant doors of bronze-clad wood are open, but as Bakabaadda walks through he learns the bulls are not the gate's only guardians. Soldiers step from both sides, bar his way with spears and ask his business. When he says he is reporting to the treasurer, one of them respectfully motions him to a stone bench and dispatches a messenger.

"Gatehouse" is a misnomer, the scribe thinks as he waits. He is in a large hall, some 80 feet square

and almost 60 feet high. In the dim light he can just make out the four fluted columns, with their twin-bull capitals, that hold up the lofty roof beams.

Suddenly three Persians appear before him; by the richness of their dress he knows them as men of rank. Bakabaadda leaps to his feet. From a small retinue of servants behind the three nobles steps a scribe carrying several parchment scrolls. Ceremoniously the scribe announces the dignitaries. They are the treasurer Vahush and two important treasury officials, Ratininda and Artataxma. Bakabaadda, speechless, bows low. His scribal colleague explains quickly that these lordly men have not come specifically to greet him but are about to make an inspection tour of the site to see how well their funds are being used. Now that Bakabaadda has arrived, they decide to put him to work immediately by having him make the rounds in their entourage. Without further conversation the party sets forth.

Outside the gatehouse's east door, flanked by another pair of colossi—bulls with human heads—the group turns left along a heavily rutted track crowded with streams of passing workers. Ahead of them a large gang of Syrian stone haulers strains against

116

thick ropes fastened to a massive section of a column set on timber rollers. They are moving the drum from the near-by quarry to a construction site. Their top foreman, called a chief-of-hundred, is exhorting them to pull harder while a lesser boss, a chief-of-ten, directs his team to rush roller logs from behind the column drum and replace them in front as the gang edges the stone forward.

The chief-of-hundred starts to bow as the officials approach, but Vahush signals him to continue so that the load's momentum will not be lost. When the treasurer comes abreast of the column drum, however, he stops, looks closely at the stone and then tells Bakabaadda to summon the chief-of-hundred. The Syrian crew stands panting from their effort while the scribe translates the conversation between their Aramaic-speaking leader and Vahush, who speaks Persian. Vahush wants to know if the quarry inspector has approved the drum. He has. Nonetheless, says Vahush, it is defective and must be replaced, and the Syrians will lose a day's pay because their chief-of-hundred should have noticed the flaw before hauling the column drum this far. The man bows submissively. Artataxma says something to Bakabaadda's fellow scribe, who takes soft clay and stylus from a pouch he carries and makes a note.

The inspection party goes through a wide, downward sloping tunnel that pierces the base of the northern fortified wall, and passes a train of Babylonians trudging up to the terrace with baskets of new sundried bricks strapped to their backs. The underpass opens on to the plain near the quarry, which swarms with hundreds of workers—Ionians, Egyptians, Sardians and Assyrians.

While Vahush studies scrolls showing designs and

Excavation of the royal complex at Persepolis was begun in 1931 by University of Chicago archaeologists and has continued under Iranian auspices. In the keyed plan below, heavy lines indicate structures charted by Americans; lighter ones, those studied by Iranians; circles and dots represent pillar locations; the striated bars, stairway placements.

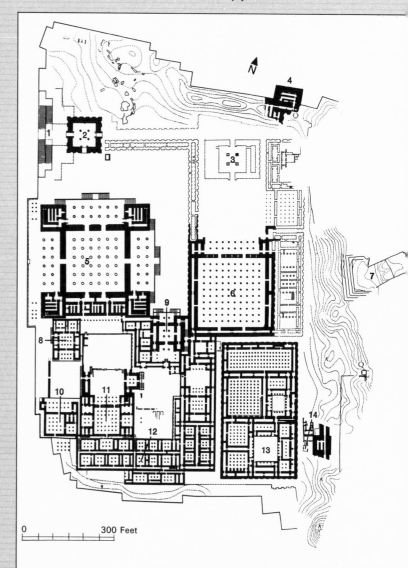

0   300 Feet

1. Stairway
2. Gate of All Lands
3. Unfinished gatehouse
4. Fortification ruins
5. Apadana (audience hall)
6. Throne hall
7. Royal tomb
8. Palace of Darius
9. Council hall
10. Palace of Artaxerxes I
11. Palace of Xerxes
12. Storerooms
13. Treasury
14. Barracks

work schedules, Bakabaadda translates the oral reports from chiefs-of-hundred who gather around Ratininda and Artataxma. The air rings with the clink and clang of busy hammers. Masons are rough-dressing bell-shaped column bases, parts of staircases, doorways and windows. As each piece is finished, the mason inscribes a symbol identifying his work team on a surface that will be hidden when the stone is put in place.

The quarry inspection completed, the treasurer's entourage returns to the terrace, passing the rejected column section, which lies abandoned where it will remain for the next 25 centuries. They turn left at the Gate of All Lands and walk east a hundred yards along a walled avenue until it issues into the north end of a vast courtyard, which is more than 100 yards long and 80 yards wide.

At the south end of the courtyard, the throne hall, the second largest structure on the terrace, is going up. Its main room will have 100 columns, although they will be only two-thirds as high as those of the apadana, which the scribe can see towering above the wall to his right. The throne hall's stone foundations have been laid and its columns are now being raised. When they are all standing and the stone doorways are in position, 10-foot-thick walls of mud brick cemented with mud mortar will be erected. Strong cedar beams will be hoisted into position, spanning outer walls and resting on the saddles of column capitals. Smaller timbers will be placed crisscross on the cedar beams and the entire grid covered by woven mats. A layer of earth three to six feet deep will be placed on the mats to complete the roof.

To reach that stage will take some years, and the scribe can readily see why as he watches a horde of labourers trying to position a single column section. The partially erected pillar already stands about 25 feet high. It is embraced by a mighty timber scaffolding from which is rigged a tackle of numerous ropes and bronze pulleys, multiplying the power of the work teams on the ground. When a column drum is finally in place, days will be consumed raising the scaffolding to a higher level before the next section can be hauled into position. And when a column is complete, workmen will spend days dismantling the scaffolding and setting it up again elsewhere.

The tour continues along the 20-foot-wide streets, up and down stairways, in and out of half-finished buildings, through mazes of rooms and passageways. In one palace Bakabaadda sees polishers patiently rubbing the dark limestone reliefs with abrasive stones until they gleam like black marble. In a street by a new building he watches men heat and crush gypsum, then mix it with clay and water to make plaster, which others will apply to floors as well as to some interior and exterior walls. Inside another structure, small and low enough so that mere log columns can be used to support the roof, workers are encasing the logs in a thick sheath of plaster to prepare them for an elaborate paint job.

The group continues towards the treasury, stopping just once to check the progress of labourers clearing silt from the underground drainage system. Walking along the terrace's easternmost street, the party passes a series of soldiers' barracks tucked in against the fortified wall. Bakabaadda wrinkles his nose. The citadel has no sewers and here, on the only part of the terrace occupied full-time by a substantial number of people and horses, the stench is oppressive.

Hearing laughter from an open door, the scribe can-

Huge Crowns for the Pillars

Among the most original features of Achaemenid buildings were the giant columns, some of them rising 65 feet—far higher than anything known to the Greeks—and terminating in massive capitals consisting of paired bulls, lions and monsters. The staggering scale of these protomas—the architectural term for such animal heads and busts—is suggested by the scene on the cover of this book. A visitor entering the main throne room at Persepolis would have seen a hundred similarly shaped capitals looming overhead, holding up the wooden roof beams and proclaiming the invincible might of the Persian Empire.

These joined bull figures once surmounted a pillar in the Persepolis palace complex. Only a few such double protomas have survived, but fragments of others indicate that the bull was a prevalent motif of the city's architecture. The sculpture is more than eight feet wide by five feet high.

This griffin, a mythical beast with an eagle's head, is one of a pair designed for a limestone capital by sculptors working for the Achaemenids. Found in an area near Persepolis that was used as a quarry and workshop, the three-foot-high head was apparently never mounted on a column crown; it may have been rejected as unsatisfactory, or fashioned to ornament a building that was never completed.

A snarling lion, part of a back-to-back sculpture similar to the bull capital opposite, made a convincing symbol of Achaemenid pride, positioned on top of one of the columns fronting Persepolis' apadana and council hall.

not resist peeking in. Off-duty soldiers sit talking and drinking. Dozens of bronze-headed spears lean against a corner and on the wall are hanging quivers packed with iron-tipped arrows and swords in scabbards. Armour and pottery field canteens are stacked on shelves. Large clay jugs, conical in shape, stand in slots cut into the floor. A soldier, rising in order to pour more wine from one of these containers, notices Bakabaadda and makes some joke at his expense. As the men laugh, Bakabaadda, embarrassed, runs to catch up with his party, which is now approaching the entrance to the treasury house.

If he was confused by the layout of the terrace at large, he is bewildered by that of the treasury, a building of more than 90,000 square feet partitioned into a maze of some 100 rooms, passages and courtyards. Even if its floor plan were simple, though, he probably would not be able to fix it in his mind, so stunned is he by the riches the interior reveals—in storerooms, workshops and offices.

He sees chambers crowded with gold and silver-plated furniture; exquisitely fashioned bowls, plates, vases and drinking vessels of gold, silver, alabaster, crystal and costly Egyptian glass. It is said, he remembers, that only a Persian who displeases the king drinks from an earthenware cup. In other rooms are sumptuous Persian carpets, ceremonial gold armour and weapons, ivory and pearls, jewellery, precious stones, frankincense, rare spices and bolts of fabulous silk, much of it dyed with the distinctive Tyrian purple reserved for royalty. Ingots of gold also lie about the treasury's working areas. Craftsmen are hard at work making gold ornamentation for statuary, as well as gold tacks, gold-headed nails and gold-plated silver wire for use in palace decorations.

In his accounting office, the tax handler ladles scoop after scoop of silver coins into a balance against a 120-karsha weight (about 22 pounds). Bakabaadda also notices some base metals: the bronze spears and swords held by the hard-eyed soldiers posted to guard the building. Recovering from his dazzled first impression of the place, the scribe reminds himself that it is not seemly to stand around gawking in such a busy place. Taken in hand by colleagues, Bakabaadda turns to the chores that will be routine for him.

He is being shown the whereabouts of styluses, pens, clay, papyrus and parchment when Artataxma sends for him. The official hands him a tightly rolled parchment bearing the clay seal of a man named Megabyzus. Bakabaadda breaks the seal and aloud translates the letter, written in Aramaic, into Persian. The document is a requisition for the wages of donkey drivers attached to the royal estate. Artataxma tells the scribe to put the payment through.

Fortunately, Bakabaadda knows the convoluted multilingual office system from similar practices at Susa. Vahush's Elamite accountants, who cannot read Aramaic, will need an authorization to pay, written in their own language, for their records. To keep it official, the authorization must be in the form of a memorandum from Artataxma to Vahush, telling him that a request for paying such and such an amount of money has been received from Megabyzus.

Bakabaadda returns to the scribes' workroom with the parchment, moulds a tablet of damp clay with two pieces of string protruding from one end and begins impressing the cuneiform characters: "To Vahush the treasurer, Artataxma says. . . ." Bakabaadda proceeds with the memorandum, including the text of

Megabyzus' letter—which requisitions "three karsha, six shekels, and two-thirds of a shekel, silver"—and finally closes with the date: "In the month of Viyaxna of the 19th year this sealed order has been given at Parsa." With the finished document in hand, the scribe returns to Artataxma, who puts his official imprimatur on the tablet.

Later, when the clay has hardened, the tablet—with the parchment letter from Megabyzus resealed and affixed to the strings—will go to the accountants. After the money has been paid, the records will be filed, still tied together, in the archives of the treasury. If the order to pay is ever challenged, the seal on the parchment will be broken and the original requisition produced.

While waiting for the tablet to dry, the scribe realizes with a sting of regret that he could have added: "Bakabaadda wrote this document." He will be sure to remember next time.

It is the first day of the first month, April, of Xerxes' 20th year. Bakabaadda has been in Parsa less than four weeks, but this has been the most eventful period of his life. Vahush has died and Ratininda has been appointed to the coveted treasurer's post. Members of the treasury staff have scarcely looked up from their records to note the changeover, so engrossed are they in preparing for the New Year's festival. Theirs was the task of organizing the preparation of appropriate regalia for the king; of pushing builders of the new treasury extension to finish the rooms for storing the tribute that would pour in from subject nations, and of purchasing wines and victuals for the feasting.

Even today, with all the preparations completed, Bakabaadda is still not free to rest, for Ratininda has asked him to stay close by during the ceremonies in case a scribe or interpreter should be needed. Bakabaadda is glad to comply; the extra duty will put him at the finest imaginable vantage point for witnessing the show, near the apadana's western portico, overlooking the plain below. The spectacle will include the appearance of the King of Kings on the terrace, a display of mounts and chariots from the monarch's stables, a procession of Persian notables and officials, and a review of delegates from subject nations bearing tribute.

Parsa is even more colourful than usual. For weeks painters have been applying fresh decoration to sculptured stone—from bas-reliefs to column capitals. Scattered over the plain are the tents of visitors, who now double the size of Parsa. Just below Bakabaadda, thousands of spectators throng Darius' pine grove, held back from the broad avenue at the foot of the terrace by a line of warriors in dress uniform. More soldiers can be seen standing in rows that stretch up the great staircase, through the Gate of All Lands and up the stairway of the apadana.

The crowd below lets loose a roar. Bakabaadda turns to see his majesty emerge from the apadana. There he is: the Great King, King of Kings, King of the Lands, Xerxes the Achaemenid, seated on a golden throne. The throne in turn is mounted on a platform, with a tasselled red canopy that sways with the measured step of its bearers: a squad of the Immortals. Xerxes wears a crimson robe and gold crown, holds a long, slender sceptre of gold and rests his blue-shod feet on a golden footstool. The red canopy is embroidered with lions, bulls and the winged symbol of his god, Ahuramazda.

The king manages to maintain his regal poise while the soldiers lower the platform to the ground. Attendants, one carrying a fly whisk made of a bull's tail and another the king's gold bow and battle-axe, step into positions behind the king, who nods his head—the sign to begin the rest of the programme.

The Elamite scribe is filled with pride to see that a hundred Susian guardsmen—recognizable by their intricately patterned gowns of yellow, turquoise blue, white and brown—lead the marchers. They are followed by grooms and horses from the royal stables and by two empty chariots—one for the king and one for the deity Ahuramazda.

Next come lords of the realm: Persian and Median dignitaries who do not march, but walk with gravity. Each Persian wears a *candys*, the characteristic flowing gown, and a fluted felt tiara. The Medes are dressed in leather trousers, tunics, laced shoes, domed felt hats and sleeved overcoats worn cape-fashion over their shoulders. Nobles of both nations are festooned with gold ornaments—ear-rings, bracelets and heavy neck rings, or torques.

When the dignitaries have passed the king, the tribute procession begins. Each delegation is guided by a Persian usher who clasps the leader of the national group by the hands. Bakabaadda, who has studied the apadana stair reliefs several times, is surprised to see that the delegations passing below him are much larger than those depicted in the reliefs. He now realizes that the sculptors were abstracting the essence of the event, while these real marchers need a lot of manpower to carry their burdens. Instead of the one sculpted dhoti-clad Indian carrying a pair of vases in baskets suspended from a yoke, dozens of Indians now approach the king. Even be-

fore the scribe can see them, he can hear in the distance gasps from the crowd, which well knows what the vases contain: pure gold dust.

A few members of each delegation bearing offerings that are personal gifts for the monarch turn off at the monumental staircase and follow the Persian and Median noblemen up through the Gate of All Lands, but most of the marchers continue along the foot of the terrace and disappear behind the northwest corner, taking their contributions directly to the treasury building by way of the tunnel entrance, which is located near the quarry.

On and on they come: Cappadocians with wagons full of elegantly embroidered clothing; Ionians with honey-rich beehives; and Susians—one leading a lioness on a leash, others carrying her cubs, still others a hoard of finely wrought weapons. With the passing of camels from Bactria and Arabia, bulls from Babylonia, wild asses from India and horses from nearly everywhere, the pall of rising dust almost reaches the privileged group on the platform. Bakabaadda is relieved when the last contingent passes and the throne on its platform is lifted again and carried into the apadana amidst cheers.

At the tail of the royal retinue, Ratininda signals Bakabaadda to follow. The bedazzled scribe steps from the sunlight into the cavernous apadana—it is big enough to hold 10,000 people—and when his eyes adjust to the relative darkness he can see before him

Bearing food, drink and utensils for the New Year's feast, a sculpted procession of servants, about 18 inches high, mounts a staircase of the council hall, or tripylon, at Persepolis. The royal entourage would first have met the king in the apadana, or audience hall, before passing through the tripylon to the annual festivities, which were held in the banquet hall.

only the transverse aisle that runs to the east door, 200 feet away, and the north-south aisle where he stands. In other directions his view is blocked by the forest of gigantic stone columns. Ratininda leads him to a place where he can discern the vague shape of throne and king. Persian monarchs, Bakabaadda knows, exploit shadowed remoteness as an important element in their kingship. A public appearance such as the one just completed outside is all the more prized for its rarity.

In the apadana, Xerxes is giving audience to the Persian and Median dignitaries; one by one they approach to address the Great King. From the few words the scribe can hear, most of the men simply repledge loyalty and state their conviction that their lord's 20th year on the throne will be one of continued glorious success. Some seem to be using the opportunity to request boons, to which the king sometimes assents with a gesture of his sceptre.

When the audience is over, Xerxes steps down from his throne and leaves through the east door, followed by the bearer of the ceremonial fly whisk and a servant holding an ornate parasol over the royal head. Xerxes' appearance on the portico is greeted once again by shouts of praise from tribute delegates and lesser Medes and Persians assembled

in the apadana's plaza, where they will be served their share of the feast. The king leads the nobles, followed at a discreet distance by their attendants, past reliefs of his father leading nobles of a previous generation and on to his new banquet hall, which is built on the terrace's highest level and is grand enough to include a central hall 75 feet square.

Only on such a public holiday, the scribe is told, does the king dine in the presence of his courtiers. At other times he eats alone, separated from his guests by curtains. At this banquet, Bakabaadda stands behind Ratininda, who is seated at a table reserved for people of his rank. The scribe has never seen such an extravagant feast—more than a thousand steers, lambs and fowl have been roasted for the occasion. An unbroken queue of royal servants files into the crowded room bringing wine, trays of fruit and covered dishes. The sounds of harp and flute accompany the proceedings, filling the hall with music.

As the meal progresses, it becomes apparent that only a tiny fraction of the food on the tables can be consumed. Later, when the king returns to the apadana to receive the tribute delegations in audience, the food that is left over will be distributed among soldiers, servants and—Bakabaadda fervently hopes—at least one scribe.

He is mentally savouring a foretaste of roast lamb adrip with rich juices when he notices a servant whispering in the treasurer's ear. Ratininda motions the scribe forward. Artataxma has sent word that the treasury staff needs help in registering the incoming royal tribute and in allocating it to the proper storerooms. Bakabaadda is to report immediately. The scribe bows, takes a last hungry glance at the repast he will not taste and departs to count up the latest increase to his king's ever-growing fortune.

The Memory of Vanished Majesty

From the heights east of Persepolis, the ruins dominate the Iranian plateau, now being farmed as far as the distant Zagros Mountains.

The ruins of Persepolis, symbol of Persian might at its zenith, rise starkly from the plain of Marv-i Dasht in southern Iran. Set on a walled terrace near the foot of a mountain, the colossal remains evoke the glory of the ceremonial capital's past.

When King Darius conceived the master plan for the complex in 520 B.C., he chose the lonely setting to lend grandeur to the elaborate sacred pageants to be held there, and to pro-vide a remote stronghold for the national treasury. His scheme de-manded perfect alignment of all structures erected on top of the 33-acre terrace, and a drainage system under-ground. The citadel was used for only a short period each year—during the New Year's festival, when emissaries from all the empire's subject nations convened to present tribute to the King of Kings. Nonetheless, each of Darius' successors added to the city's magnificence. By the time it was sacked by the Greek conqueror Alex-ander in 330 B.C., Persepolis' man-made platform was entirely covered with buildings.

A German architect, Friedrich Krefter, who first studied the site in the 1930s, recently made the drawings that are matched with the photo-graphs on the following pages to show Persepolis as it looked at the peak of its splendour in the Fifth Century B.C.

Two 18-foot limestone bulls, one now headless, flank the doorway of Persepolis' official entrance. Named the Gate of All Lands by King Xerxes, who commissioned it around 475 B.C., the portal originally had wooden doors. The 60-foot columns beyond the access held the roof of an anteroom.

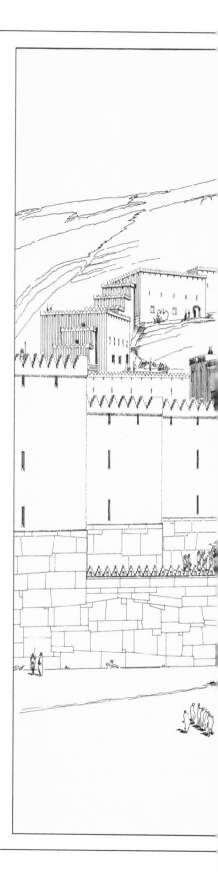

From the Gate of All Lands (outlined in red to correspond with the detail on the left), a double reversing stairway led down from the terrace on which Persepolis was built, 46 feet above the Marv-i Dasht Plain. This foundation of stone and dirt was reinforced by a retaining wall of massive limestone blocks. On top of the wall, which curved around the perimeter of the city, were fortresses and guard towers (background) of mud brick. The audience hall, or apadana, is to the right of the gate.

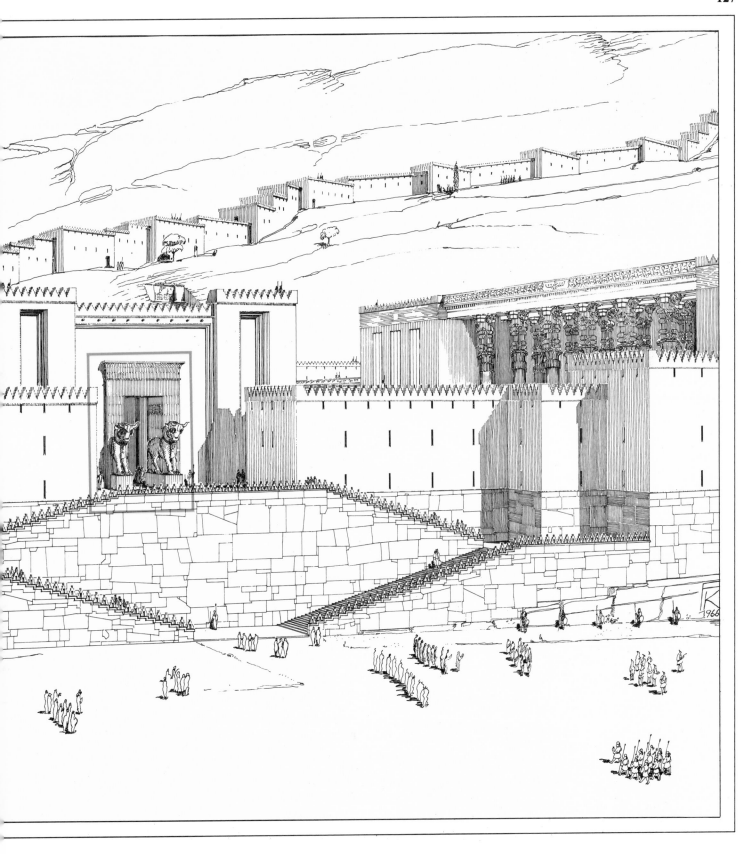

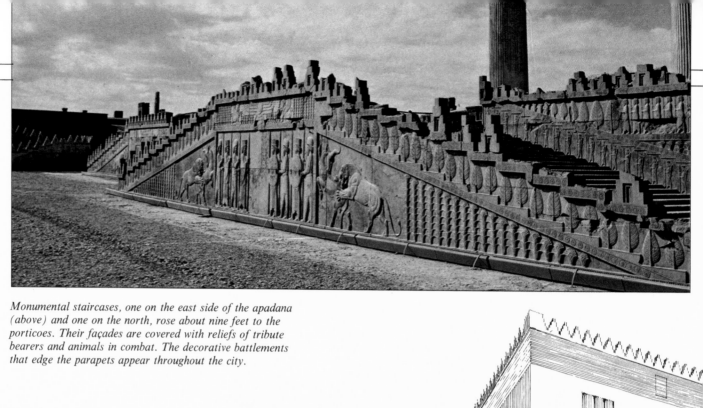

Monumental staircases, one on the east side of the apadana
(above) and one on the north, rose about nine feet to the
porticoes. Their façades are covered with reliefs of tribute
bearers and animals in combat. The decorative battlements
that edge the parapets appear throughout the city.

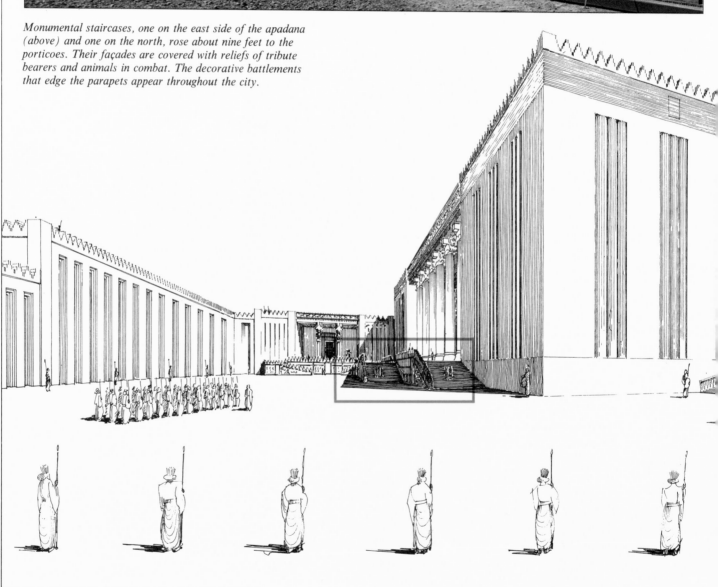

Once inside the citadel's walls, guests and dignitaries who visited Persepolis found themselves in an open square before the apadana. From there, anyone who had business with the king was ushered into the great audience hall via the northern staircase and portico (at centre, below). After the visitors had assembled, the king himself entered through the eastern doorway (outlined in red to match the photograph opposite). Of the two almost identical stairways—one built by Darius, the other by Xerxes—the eastern one is more intact; it was protected by a blanket of rubble until excavation in 1932.

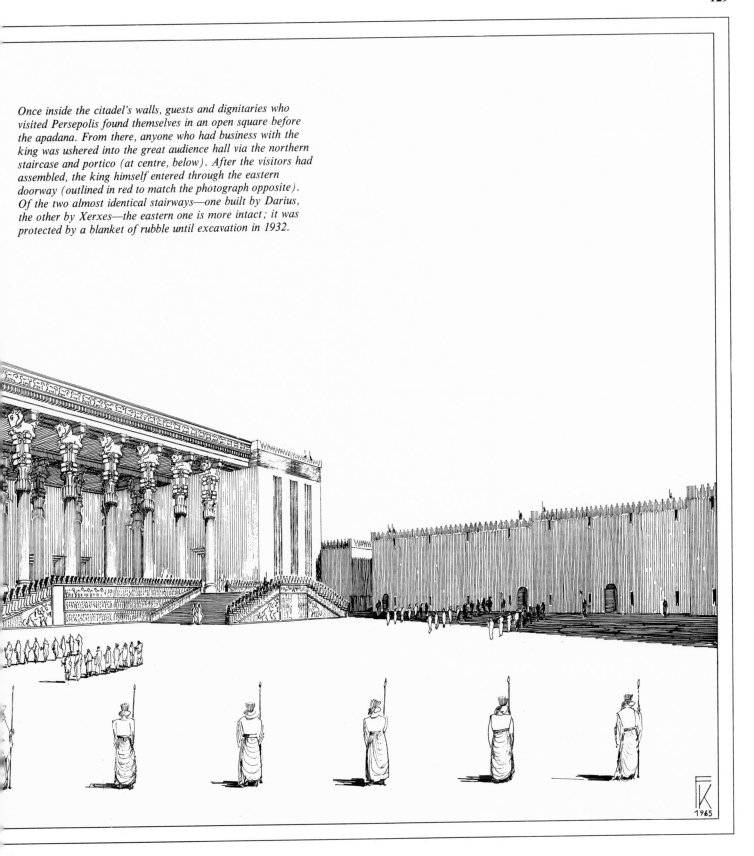

Five of the surviving slender limestone columns of the apadana rise more than 65 feet. They once held the audience hall's massive wooden roof beams. The two pillars to the left, part of the western portico, were set on fluted, bell-shaped stone bases. The three to the right, resting on simple square blocks, were inside the structure. Originally there were 72 columns in the building; only 13 still stand.

At the edge of the western portico of the apadana, the king sat elevated on his portable throne while reviewing the New Year's procession. The 197-foot-wide colonnade—one of three opening from the hall—permitted light to enter the dim interior of the great building. Each had 12 columns topped by a double-bull capital. Longitudinal beams of cedar from Lebanon supported the roof's lighter cross timbers.

When Xerxes inherited the Persian Empire in 486 B.C., the favour of Ahuramazda seemed boundless and the future of the Achaemenids bright indeed. In an easy and peaceful transition, the 35-year-old crown prince had received the mantle and titles of royalty as the rightful heir of Darius the Great, who had lived out his years with honour and died a natural death.

As it turned out, Xerxes was to be the last Great King to take the throne under such auspicious conditions. By the end of his 22-year reign, the lack of thought his predecessors had given to the matter of succession came to plague the monarchy. In all, six Achaemenids followed Xerxes, and the ascension of each was tainted with intrigue and bloodshed. With but one exception, the succeeding Great Kings were weak men who lacked the stature and fibre of the empire's founders. As a result, the final 13 decades of Achaemenid rule witnessed the devastation of what had been the ancient world's greatest agglomeration of power.

The decay, however, primarily affected the political system and the administrative core in the Persian homeland; in the satrapies the intellectual pursuits of men flourished. Their activity was nurtured in the atmosphere of stability—the respite from war and upheaval—that Cyrus II had established and Darius I consolidated. Even after their reigns, this climate continued to prevail in the outlying parts of the empire, and contributed significantly to scientific advances;

The still-vivid memory of ancient Persia's past glory inspired this 10th Century A.D. miniature illustrating an epic poem about the lineage of Persian kings. In this apocryphal version of the end of the Achaemenid Dynasty in 330 B.C., Darius III dies in the lap of the Greek conqueror Alexander—represented as Darius' long-lost Persian half brother.

in Babylon, Egypt and Ionia, priestly scholars contemplated the heavens and charted the constellations and movements of the solar system, laying the foundations of modern astronomy and mathematics. The impotence and corruption of the later Achaemenids never disrupted this intellectual ferment.

Many explanations have been advanced for the Achaemenids' political decline. The contemporary Greeks, whose own fortunes were rising at Persia's expense, were too close to the events of the empire's turnabout to view the situation objectively, but they were the first to offer a theory about what was going on. The Persians, Greek historians reckoned, had offended the gods. In the Classical view, the Persians had grown soft and licentious in their personal lives, rendering themselves unfit to fight or to govern; they had also betrayed their divine trust—the hegemony in Asia that the Greeks conceded to them—in order to trespass in Europe, territory the gods had bestowed upon the Greeks.

The theory has some merit, especially where it touches on the Persians' hedonism. But more concrete factors than the comparative oral tone of the Greeks and the Achaemenids were at work pulling down the Persian imperial structure. Separatism—the thrust of culturally and geographically distinct satrapies and subsatrapies to re-establish their own political identities—was a persistent threat to the empire's stability. A man of Darius' stature could hold such separatist forces in check, but the increasing repressiveness of the later kings had a negative effect in countering these internal challenges. As ever-mounting taxes dismantled the prosperity that had once made the relationships of the satrapies with the empire worthwhile for all parties, the resulting resentment festered into outright revolts. The later Achaemenid rulers responded with acts of brutality that only agitated the rebellious spirits they sought to quell.

Furthermore, even while the Achaemenids' internal problems were accumulating, they were also being confronted increasingly by the Greeks, whose power had multiplied greatly since Cyrus the Great, at the outset of his imperial campaigns, had crushed Croesus of Lydia. Cyrus had found it easy to pluck the neighbouring Greek-colonized city-states of Asia Minor, one by one, without so much as a protest from their brethren in European Greece. But when Darius launched his punitive expedition against the Scythians in about 513 B.C., he had first to cross through the Greek world. Most of the city-states of Greece submitted quietly to the invasion, though Athens and Eretria bided their time and in 499 B.C. provided men and ships to the lost Ionian cities when they revolted against Persia.

The assistance was unavailing; the Ionians succeeded in doing little damage to Persia beyond burning down the satrapal capital of Sardis. Darius deported the troublemakers, imposed punishments upon the cities and shrewdly replaced some of the most unpopular of the tyrants who had been running Ionian affairs on his behalf. At first glance, the revolt had seemed to matter little. But as events would show, both sides in the affair found their appetites whetted for more conflict. The Greco-Persian Wars, which were to last 50 years, had begun.

To retaliate for the burning of Sardis, Darius made preparations for a seaborne assault on Greece itself. While troops were being gathered and ships outfitted, he sent envoys from Greek city to Greek city demanding voluntary submission. Some succumbed to the pressure; Sparta, Athens and Eretria refused, and Sparta and Athens forged an alliance against the Persian threat. The Great King can only have been amused. He relished a fight and he knew that the Greeks had never been able to count on one another.

By the summer of 490 B.C. he was ready to exact his revenge. A 25,000-man Persian army, transported by 600 ships, invaded Greece intending to concentrate its attack on the cities that had refused to submit. As Darius had foreseen, his enemies were only partially prepared for the invasion. Betrayed from within by Persian sympathizers, Eretria was smashed in six days. The Persian fleet next put in at the Bay of Marathon, and the army prepared for a day's march south to Athens.

The Athenians had no choice but to attack the Persian forces before the enemy could surround the city and isolate it from its Spartan allies. On August 12, 490 B.C., the heavily armed Athenian infantry charged at Marathon. The assault drove the invaders back to their ships. Without hesitation, the Greeks followed them into the water, grabbing the vessels' anchor cables to keep them from getting away; seven of the ships were captured. The next day the Persians made a second fruitless attempt to take Athens by sea, only to discover that the tireless Athenians had marched home on the double and were preparing to take them on again. Demoralized, the Persian expedition, now reduced by 6,400 casualties, headed back to the safety of imperial territory.

The Battle of Marathon surprised the Greeks as much as it did the Persians. The Persians were no longer invincible—either in their own minds or in the opinion of their enemies. Even as they were considering how to avenge this critical loss, two pivotal events within the empire intervened: a major revolt in Egypt in October 486 B.C. and the death of Darius the Great the very next month.

When Darius died at the age of 64, he had reigned for 36 years. Now, at this historic moment in Persian history, Crown Prince Xerxes was entrusted with a titanic task. Turning his back for several years on the problems posed by the new Greek strength, Xerxes marshalled the full weight of his imperial armies against the Egyptian rebellion—apparently the first in a series of such revolts prompted by a rise in tax levies—and against another eruption in Babylonia in 482 B.C.

Xerxes acted vigorously, punishing the two satrapies harshly for their insurgency. Both countries lost the privileged status they had once enjoyed as imperial civilizations in their own right. In place of tolerance and a judicious amount of local autonomy, Xerxes thereafter used naked force as the instrument of his rule in those regions. Then, when Xerxes had finished these police actions and was ready once more to use the same strong-arm methods on the Greeks, he announced: "I shall pass through Europe from end to end and make it all one country."

Nearly four years went into preparations for the invasion. Herodotus calculated the grand total of the Persian land army at 1.7 million troops backed up by 3,000 fully manned fighting ships and transports. Obviously, a Greek would wish to portray his countrymen as if they were David opposing Persia's Goliath, inflating the oppressor's numbers accordingly; modern historians think the actual figures were closer to 200,000 Persian soldiers and 1,200 ships. Nevertheless, the aggregate was still the largest military force the ancient world had yet seen.

Engineers anchored two bridges of boats across the Hellespont, the strait where Europe and Asia approach within three-quarters of a mile. A storm broke up the bridge before the army had a chance to use them and Xerxes, furious at what seemed the insolence of nature, had the Hellespont lashed 300 times, branded with hot irons and fettered by the symbolic act of throwing a pair of shackles into the water. After a second pair of bridges was completed, in the spring of 480 B.C., Xerxes' host crossed over to the European shore.

The Persians soon discovered that campaigning with so large an army had severe drawbacks. In addition to the sheer cumbrousness of the expedition, its mixture of nationalities, languages, weapons, fighting techniques and customs hindered efficient command. The army had also grown to like its comforts. The Ten Thousand Immortals now travelled in a manner that would have shocked their counterparts in the old days of hard fighting and hard living. Herodotus said that among the native Persians "every man glittered with gold, which he carried about his person in unlimited quantity. They were accompanied, moreover, by covered carriages full of their women and servants, all elaborately fitted out."

The time Xerxes had lost with all his planning and ponderous bridge construction proved costly, for it permitted the Greeks a generous period in which to build their defence. For the first time, Sparta was able to form a Greek war coalition—30 states, all of which agreed to cease their own squabbles for the duration of the crisis—and to muster two co-ordinated forces: one on land under the leadership of King Leonidas of

Sparta, the other at sea under his countryman Eurybiades. Assessing their military position with unprecedented professionalism, the Greeks chose a battleground favourable to themselves—a site deep in their own territory at Thermopylae.

A narrow coastal gateway through the mountains to Attica and thus to Athens, Thermopylae was to be the scene of a holding action, blocking the Persian host while the Greek fleet maintained surveillance over the enemy's navy to the east, near the island of Euboea. Xerxes reached Thermopylae in early August to find a small army of 7,000 preparing to defend the pass. He paused for four days, expecting the outnumbered Greeks to withdraw at any moment.

On the fifth day, his patience exhausted, he sent in the Medes to winkle out the enemy. In the confines of the 50-foot-wide defile, numbers made little difference; and the Spartans, who were at the forefront of the Greek formation, stubbornly held their ground. After several hours Xerxes ordered the badly mauled Medes to withdraw and—to make a quick job of it—called on his Immortals. When night came they, too, were compelled to pull back, no more successful than the Medes. The next day the Immortals attacked again and once more failed to dislodge the Spartans.

Possibly Xerxes was developing some doubts about the whole expedition when a Greek traitor showed the Persians a little-known path that would take them over the mountain and bring them around behind the Greek position. When King Leonidas became aware of the impending encirclement, he ordered most of his troops to withdraw south to the Isthmus of Corinth, where the Greek allies had agreed to gather for the main defence. Meanwhile, he and 300 of his own Spartans sacrificed their lives to delay Xerxes. During these actions, the Greek and Persian fleets engaged indecisively off Euboea.

After mopping up Leonidas' rear guard at Thermopylae, Xerxes marched unopposed to Athens, which he reached at the end of August. On orders from Themistocles, Athens' military leader, the city had been abandoned by all but a handful of men who held the Acropolis, the fortified hill with its great temple that overlooked the town. Overcoming this pitiful resistance, the Persians looted the temple and burned all the Acropolis' buildings. News of the victory was sped by royal post riders to Susa where, said Herodotus, Persians "strewed the roads with myrtle-boughs, burned incense and gave themselves up to every sort of pleasure and merrymaking".

But the celebrations were to be short-lived. The citizens of Susa would soon receive news that, Herodotus reported with pride, made them "weep and wail in unappeasable grief".

As the Persian armies concentrated on the mainland, the imperial fleet warily drew close to the much smaller Greek navy, which had withdrawn to the waters near the island of Salamis, there to defend the Athenians, who had sought refuge on it. The island is separated from the coast by a narrow strait, in which the Greek fleet had taken station. Some of its admirals, influenced by the divisiveness that always plagued the Greek cause, were restless; they wanted to sail home to protect their own cities rather than fight in defence of the Athenians—off the coast of Athenian territories that were already occupied by the Persians.

But a determined Themistocles took charge. First, he convinced the unhappy Greek admirals that their only real chance of staving off defeat at home was to beat the Persians here and now; and second, he set the battle in motion by leaking word to the enemy that the Greeks were demoralized and therefore could be easily destroyed if they were engaged immediately in the strait.

The ruse worked. The Persians blocked both ends of the narrows and sailed in to attack. Xerxes, confident of victory, sat down to watch the action from a portable throne set up on shore. But the narrowness of the quarters between mainland and island put the Persians at a serious disadvantage. In a sense, the Battle of Salamis was analogous to the land contest at Thermopylae; in the channel the superior numbers of the imperial fleet—including Egyptian, Phoenician and Ionian vessels—had less effect than the superior

tactics and more manoeuvrable ships of the Greeks. Persia's allies massed in such a way that they continually fouled one another. The Greeks, however, worked in concert; they used their stout vessels to ram the enemy ships and then board them in order to dispatch the marines and oarsmen.

The mêlée became a rout. The beach at Xerxes' feet was soon littered with the wreckage of his ships and the bodies of his men. Persian ships lucky enough to escape hastened a few miles east to Phaleron on the mainland, where they were pulled ashore under the protection of the Persian land forces. The Greeks towed their fewer crippled vessels to Salamis. Certain that the Persians would come back, they prepared to fight again.

But Xerxes was no longer thinking along aggressive lines. He feared the victorious Greeks might sail for the Hellespont and destroy his bridges, cutting off his life line to Asia. With winter coming on—it was now October—he ordered what remained of his fleet to withdraw to the Hellespont and take up defensive positions around his bridges. Leaving Mardonius, his leading general, in Greece with a third of the Persian army, Xerxes and the main body withdrew, halting only long enough to detach one contingent in Thrace to guard communications lines, then proceeding with the men who were left to Ionia where a new revolt threatened. At the straits Xerxes found the bridge had once again been destroyed by storms; he had to call on his reduced navy to ferry his soldiers to safety.

Mardonius, spending the winter of 480-479 B.C. in Thessaly, did his best to split the Greek war coalition by diplomacy. But his measures failed, largely through the steadfastness of the Spartans, who stiffened the backs of the Athenians when the latter

The monumental tombs of (left to right) Darius II, Artaxerxes I and Darius I were hewn into a cliff just north of Persepolis at Naqsh-i Rustam. Their cross-shaped designs, embellished with sculpted figures, follow the pattern initiated by Darius I, whose tomb façade is 75 feet high and 61 feet wide—dimensions best appreciated by noting the persons walking at lower right. Each sepulchre has a door leading to interior vaults. The carvings at the bases of the tombs were added in the Third Century A.D., at the time of the Sasanian Empire.

seemed about to accept Mardonius' offer of territory and Persian support. The Spartans pulled together a confederated Greek force and decisively defeated Mardonius at the Battle of Plataea on the 27th of August, 479 B.C. The very same day, far away on the Ionian coast of Asia Minor, the Greek navy landed warriors at Mycale, where some of Xerxes' surviving ships and men had come to rest the preceding autumn. Once again the Greeks made short work of the Persians and finished the job of subverting the loyalty of their already insurgent Ionian city-state vassals. The battles of Plataea and Mycale marked the disastrous finish of the Great King's ambitious undertaking. By the end of Xerxes' reign in 465 B.C. the Persians no longer could claim even a toe hold in Europe. The era of imperial expansion was over.

The long-term significance of Persia's defeat was not apparent to the Achaemenids. Xerxes could still comfort himself with the certainty that his realm remained the world's greatest power. In terms of territory, the loss of Greece was negligible, and the Great King, now in the seventh year of his reign, complacently resumed the conduct of peacetime affairs. Henceforth, Xerxes showed little interest in grand designs, retiring to the seclusion of his palaces.

Xerxes' reign ended in a manner that was to become traditional among Achaemenids. Through the machinations of the commander of the palace guard and the royal chamberlain, Xerxes was murdered in his bed in 465 B.C. In that year, Persia's fortunes were delivered into the hands of a series of kings who combined, in differing proportions, the faults of invidiousness with political and military ineptitude. Under them, in 135 years—a period slightly longer than that of the empire's extraordinary rise—Persia withered and weakened.

The 40-year reign of Artaxerxes I, Xerxes' successor, reinforced the patterns that were rotting the empire from within. To start, he acquired his power violently, for he was not the legitimate heir to the throne; his elder brother, the more likely successor, had to be eliminated first.

Artaxerxes' successors outdid him in personal ruthlessness. Darius II pushed court decadence to its limits. The casualties of his murderous ascension included several siblings, who were dispatched by such ghoulish means as stoning and being baked slowly in an oven. One was plied with rich food and strong drink, hoisted above a bed of hot coals and perched precariously on a narrow beam, whence he eventually plummeted drunkenly to his death.

The rule of the next Great King, Artaxerxes II, was marred by yet another rebellion in the satrapies, whose leaders for the first time tried to band together to put an end to Achaemenid power. They almost succeeded, but internal discord in one subject nation weakened the already loose coalition of satrapies; the rebellion's collapse temporarily rescued the Persians' dignity. Thus in 358 B.C. a third Artaxerxes made a stab at reassuring his dynasty's authority.

For a brief time under Artaxerxes III, Persia's declining fortunes were reversed. In a series of desperate stands, for which many Greek mercenaries had to be recruited, Artaxerxes managed to put down revolts in the satrapies of Phoenicia and Syria and to regain a foothold in lower Egypt after an uprising there.

But a true resuscitation of the empire's lost vigour was cut short by the king's death. In 338 B.C. an ambitious court eunuch named Bagoas, whose purpose

was to put upon the throne a weakling whom he could manipulate, poisoned Artaxerxes. After two more years of intrigue, Bagoas was able to murder the next in line—Arses III—as well as his entire family. Finally, in 336 B.C., one of Artaxerxes' grandnephews succeeded in getting Bagoas to drink one of his own draughts of poison. The poisoner was the man who was to distinguish himself in history as the last Achaemenid: Darius III.

When Darius III began his reign, the great imperial system developed by the first Darius was as soiled by corruption and maladministration as the Achaemenid throne was stained with blood. Egypt and the satrapies of western Asia fumed under a harsh rule. Babylonia had been taxed into a state of advanced economic decay; once-thriving cities were virtually abandoned. Persia thus seemed ripe for a full-scale Greek invasion. In 336 B.C. a 20-year-old named Alexander of Macedonia forged an army and prepared to hurl his spear into the oil of Asia.

Accompanied by about 35,000 Macedonians and Greeks, Alexander ferried across the Hellespont in the spring of 334 B.C. They were met a few miles to the east on the shore of the river Granicus by the Persian satraps of Asia Minor at the head of an army that was numerically superior to Alexander's. The Persians fought valiantly; many satraps and nobles were killed. But the toughness, discipline and tactical cunning that once had characterized Persian soldiery were now the attributes of the enemy, who stormed across the river to smash the defenders. For the empire, one of the most disastrous effects of the defeat was the loss in battle of a large proportion of its Greek mercenaries, the best soldiers it had.

Alexander easily occupied all of Asia Minor in the course of the next year. In 333 B.C. he marched south into Syria where Darius III, with an army half again as large as the invader's, awaited him. They met in November near the town of Issus on a narrow coastal plain bounded by sea and mountains. The contest was still very much in the balance when the Achaemenid king fled in panic, abandoning not only his army but his mother, wife and infant heir. On witnessing their king's cowardice, the Persian troops broke ranks and ran. The victorious Alexander took Darius' family under his personal protection.

As the conqueror continued south through Syria, Darius sent him a peace bid: he would yield all the empire west of the Euphrates. Alexander, determined to have everything, rejected the offer. Meeting strong resistance along the way only from the cities of Tyre and Gaza, the Macedonian entered Egypt in triumph and accepted its crown near the end of 332 B.C. The next year he turned east, towards the empire's heart.

Darius, having assembled another huge army, was ready to make a final stand in Mesopotamia. But instead of the natural defensive barrier of the river Tigris, he chose a less advantageous spot near Gaugamela, four days' journey to the east. The armies clashed on October 1, 331 B.C. Again Darius took

142

Darius III (centre), last of the Achaemenid kings, confronts a helmetless Alexander of Macedonia at the Battle of Issus in 333 B.C. In his chariot, Darius wears a look of terror as the invincible Greek charges a phalanx of Persian lancers; a riderless horse (foreground) shies in panic. The scene was rendered in mosaic in the First Century B.C. for a floor at Pompeii, where lava damaged it.

fright before the battle's outcome was clear, and ran.

From then on—though Darius remained a potential threat and would eventually have to be done away with—Alexander had only to pick up his prizes. In Babylon he showed himself a better student of Cyrus the Great than that king's own Achaemenid heir; he ordered the restoration of the temple dedicated to the god Bel-Marduk. At Susa he emptied his first fabulous Persian royal treasury.

Persepolis was surrendered to Alexander by its garrison commander without a fight, but the conqueror sacked the city nonetheless, in revenge for Xerxes' destruction of Athens. Securing the terrace with its palaces and treasury, the young Greek turned loose his Macedonians on the lower city. For an entire day they murdered the men, carried off the women and plundered the houses.

Looting the state treasury required a more methodical approach, so rich was the trove. Alexander sent back to Babylon and Susa for extra mules and camels to carry the spoils away. While awaiting the completion of this business, he visited near-by Pasargadae, where he claimed more treasure.

Classical writers gave varying accounts of what happened in the magnificent capital during its final day of existence. One chronicler said Alexander publicly announced he was going to burn Persepolis as an act of vengeance. Others said Alexander and his officers were enjoying a last drunken party in one of the terrace's palaces when a beautiful courtesan named Thais urged him to "let the hands of women make short shrift of the glories of the Persians"—meaning that she wanted permission to set fires. Whether Alexander thought of it himself or got the idea from Thais, torches were unquestionably applied.

The conflagration was soon intense. In the throne hall, stone carvings of bearded Persian soldiers stood immobile while flames licked along the rafters of the building they symbolically guarded. At last the earthen roof came crashing down. Fire roared up the high corner towers of the apadana as if they were chimney flues. The stone column bases of the treasury cracked and bundles of iron spear- and arrowheads stored there were fused together as their shafts burned away. The loft that housed the archives collapsed, spilling clay tablets on to the floor of the room below, while parchment records vanished into smoke.

Even before the fires died, Alexander and his main force set out for Ecbatana to unburden yet another royal treasury. By this time, his haul of silver and gold

from Persepolis alone was estimated to total 180,000 talents—about 5,500 tons—of silver. Then the conqueror pushed on to the northeast in pursuit of Darius. Alexander soon found him—dead, assassinated by a Persian satrap who evidently feared that his king would capitulate. Alexander had the body sent back to Persepolis for burial while he and his armies mopped up. After six more years of campaigning against tribes in the northeastern provinces, his conquest was total. The vast world that had been the Achaemenids' was now Greek.

The razing of Persepolis, the looting of the treasuries, the murder of the last Achaemenid and the capture of all the lands that had once been Persia's were not enough for the many chauvinists among the victors; some even sought to assume the mantle of Persia's greatness by insisting that the Persians were actually of Greek stock. But others, more level-headed, let credit be given where it was due and acknowledged that they inherited from the various nations of the Persian Empire an invaluable legacy on which they were to build much of Western culture.

The world that Persia had controlled was a perpetual source of fascination for the intellectually omnivorous Greeks. Even before Alexander's conquest, countless Hellenic scholars had travelled east to what they knew were centres of learning in Egypt and Babylonia. Some even went as far as the Persian homeland itself. Among those inveterate searchers after wisdom early in the Fourth Century B.C., while Artaxerxes II was king, was the philosopher Plato. Though incessant wars prevented him from ever reaching Iran, Plato did go as far as Egypt in pursuing his curiosity. In the philosopher's earliest book, *First Alcibiades*, Plato demonstrated a substantial acquaintance with the customs, methods of education and religion of the Persians. And some scholars contend that the ethical dualism revealed in some of Plato's later philosophical treatises derived originally from the conflict between good and evil that was fundamental to the tenets of Zoroaster.

Indeed, the region dominated by the Persians had been the source of most of the advances on which civilization rests: the development of agriculture, urban society, metallurgy and writing. It was also the cradle of science. In Mesopotamia, the discipline of studying the nature of the universe was already more than two millennia old when the Achaemenids came to power. And elsewhere in the Middle East, especially in Egypt and Anatolia, there were venerable traditions of astronomical and mathematical study that came under the hegemony of the Great Kings.

It is true that Cyrus the Great and his followers were not personally attracted in marked degree to the lofty preoccupations of the learned men in their satrapies. They were drawn principally to whatever appeared to offer practical advantages; most science in the ancient world would have seemed highly abstract to the Persian kings, except where it related to such administrative realities as the reckoning of time. But the Achaemenids did not discourage these apparently obscure investigations as other, less tolerant empire builders had been known to do.

Even in the enlightened Athens of the Fifth Century B.C., glorying in its golden age under Pericles, studies of the cosmos were legally banned as blasphemous—and the penalty for defying the ban could be rigorous. This was brought home to one astronomer who considered himself a Greek. Anaxagoras was a native of the city of Clazomenae, in Persian-ruled Ionia, who settled in Athens. There he stood trial for impiety. Anaxagoras' theories included many ideas about the heavenly bodies that were anathema to the ethnocentric Athenians. For example, Anaxagoras proposed that the sun was a body of red-hot metal even bigger than the Peloponnesus, which is about 110 miles across. For this (and also for harbouring Persian sympathies in the Greco-Persian power contest) Anaxagoras was driven into exile.

A contrasting attitude was evident in Persia during the same period. Darius the Great was summoning scholars from Babylonia to help refine the calendar, according to which Persians scheduled such all-important pageants as the New Year's rite. It was in this sort of endeavour that the astronomers of Babylonia confronted the apparent capriciousness and disharmony in the movements of heavenly bodies. They tried to comprehend why lunar eclipses occurred at what seemed to be erratic intervals, why planets and bright stars disappeared for mysterious lengths of time and moved in unexpected directions and why the equinoxes did not occur on precisely the same days each year.

The motive for probing these perplexing phenomena was, of course, originally religious; in the ancient world the intentions of the gods—believed to be residents of the sky—were expressed in the changing conformations of celestial bodies. It was traditionally the function of temple priests, therefore, to figure out what divinely ordained events the gods had in store for their worshippers. Thus the priests watched the sky intensely and, in mathematical terms, methodically recorded what they saw. Temple storehouses in Babylonia contained clay tablets incised with cuneiform script covering literally centuries of continuously observed occurrences. These records furnished what modern scientists call working data—the essential body of information, gathered regularly over a long period, that provides the basis for theoretical conclusions about nature.

In the First Millennium B.C., especially during the period of general stability while the Achaemenids ruled the Middle East, Babylonia's priests added to their data and put it to work. They established the cyclically recurrent placement of planets and stars in the heavens, and the manner in which eclipses occur at definite intervals. They came to realize that countless variations might take place within a given period, but that eventually any sequence of heavenly events was bound to repeat itself. With such knowledge came the ability to predict, by mathematical calculation, what celestial events would come to pass in both the near and the very distant future. Thus the holy men of Babylonia became the fathers of astronomical science.

One scientific investigator who was mentioned by Classical writers, and who flourished under the Great Kings, was the astronomer Nabu-rimanni, a resident of Babylon during the reign of Darius I. Some of Nabu-rimanni's original data recorded on clay still survive; others can be studied from a copy of his works made in Persia during the Third Century A.D. This text asserts that Nabu-rimanni made accurate predictions of lunar and solar eclipses, plotted the moon's phases so that they could be forecast and measured the ranging lengths of days with extraordinary precision. There are remarkably few discrepancies between what Nabu-rimanni—working without a telescope or modern mathematical techniques or even a proper mechanical clock—calculated 24 centuries ago and what modern astronomers, armed with sophisticated optical equipment and computers, can determine. Between Nabu-rimanni's day and the turn of the 20th Century, only one celestial observer was able to compute the periods of heavenly bodies with greater precision—and he was another Babylonian. His name was Kidinnu—called Cidenas by the Greeks, who recognized his brilliance—and he worked around 375 B.C., during the reign of Artaxerxes II.

Babylonian innovation in astronomy attracted the attention of, and personal visits from, fellow scientists in Greece. One of the most distinguished guests was the astronomer-philosopher Democritus of Abdera, whose curiosity took him exploring throughout Asia Minor, Egypt and Mesopotamia. He returned to Athens fully grounded in Babylonian science, which provided the basis for one of the first theorems in solid geometry. Democritus also introduced to Greece the Babylonian methods for calculating the positions of constellations, as well as the idea that the earth has north and south poles. On this firm scientific foundation, Democritus also built the hypothesis that all matter was made up of infinitesimally small, indestructible particles of irreducible size: atoms.

Another notable Greek to profit from scientific learning in the Persian Empire was Pythagoras, one of the founders of modern geometry. The source of his knowledge, however, was probably not Babylonia but that region's long-time competitor as a centre of learning: Egypt. As distinguished in their own right as the Babylonians for achievements in astronomy and mathematics, Egypt's priests, too, played host-tutor to scholars from Greece—including Plato and Thales; the latter brought home with him to Athens the revolutionary Egyptian idea that a year should be measured as 365 days.

After Alexander's conquest of the Persian world, the succeeding generations of mathematicians and astronomers were predominantly Greek. The roster included such influential and familiar personalities as Eudoxus, Euclid, Archimedes and Ptolemy. These men were the direct intellectual descendants of the patient and brilliant holy men of the Middle East who had created the discipline of science.

The work of the ancients was thus not discarded. Its value was particularly evident to Alexander, who yearned to knit together the Greek and Persian worlds. The conqueror admired much of what he brought under Greek dominion. He adopted the Persian system of administration, included Persian military units and Persian commanders in his army, and arranged a mass wedding between his highest officers and Persian noblewomen. He himself married a daughter of King Darius III's. He even began to dress in the Persian style. Under him, the heritage of the ancient world was firmly incorporated in the new spirit of Hellenism.

The transfer of science from East to West is symbolic of the total shift that occurred in the centuries following the crucial date of 330 B.C. That period marked the end of three millennia of western Asian mastery over human civilization and the beginning of a thousand years of European domination. The Persians' contribution to this evolutionary process had been indirect but crucial: under a single political unit they fused together all the great, diffuse cultural gifts that had emerged in the Middle East and passed them on—intact and at their peak—to Western man.

Heirs to the Mantle of Cyrus

With the conquests of Alexander the Great, a wave of Greek influence swept through the lands once subject to the Achaemenid kings. That was followed early in the Christian Era by increasing pressure from Rome. But many Achaemenid traditions survived this Western tide to be inherited by other Middle Eastern rulers.

Most notable among these heirs were the Parthians, who rose to dominance in Persia in the Second Century B.C., and the Sasanians, who overthrew the Parthians about 400 years later and eventually built an empire rivalling the Achaemenids'.

The Parthians kept alive the Zoroastrian faith, and the Sasanians made it their official creed. Monarchs in both lines legitimized their rule by claiming descent from the Persian sovereigns and assuming the Achaemenid title King of Kings. Furthermore, stone reliefs memorializing Parthian and Sasanian rulers not only echoed motifs found in the art of the original Persians, but some were carved into the very cliffs containing the tombs of the Achaemenid kings.

This eight-foot effigy of Antiochus I, who ruled a small Anatolian kingdom during the First Century B.C., lies before his tomb at Nemrud Dagh, a site in southeast Turkey. He claimed to be a direct descendant of Darius the Great.

The Parthians: Old Values Restored

The vitality of the Achaemenid legacy is powerfully demonstrated in the coins, reliefs and other relics of Parthian kings who ruled Persia from about 170 B.C. to A.D. 224. These monarchs were descended from semi-nomadic Iranian tribesmen who, around the middle of the Third Century B.C., established a kingdom in the former Achaemenid satrapy of Parthia in northeastern Iran. Thereafter, the Parthians became sovereigns of an empire that reached from the river Oxus eastwards to the Euphrates, where their armies blocked aggressive Roman advances into the Middle East.

Increasingly impressed by their own power, the kings of Parthia came to look upon themselves as true successors to the mighty Cyrus, Darius and Xerxes. By the First and Second centuries A.D. they had succeeded in asserting their Achaemenid ancestry as official doctrine. They had also begun to reject the Hellenization of Persian life initiated in the time of Alexander—a turnabout that opened the way for the restoration of Achaemenid values, especially in art and religion.

This portrait of Zoroaster was probably made during the Third Century A.D. at the Syrian town of Dura-Europos—a Parthian outpost that the Romans captured in A.D. 154. The fact that the painting was executed after the Roman conquest indicates that the creed survived in spite of the Parthians' ouster.

The reverse side (left) of a First Century B.C. gold coin struck by Mithridates II of Parthia bears the figure of Arsaces, who founded the Parthian Dynasty; he holds a bow, as do the archers imprinted on Persian coinage (page 73). Mithridates appears on the obverse with a long Achaemenid-style beard.

Horizontal registers of this rock carving from the Second or Third Century B.C. represent the investiture of Abar-Basi, King of Elymais, a Parthian vassal state in southern Iran. The ceremony, with the enthroned king flanked by rows of courtiers and captives, mimics the relief of Darius the Great at Behistun (pages 29 and 31). The larger figure (left) worshipping at a fire altar is Orodes, Abar-Basi's successor.

The Sasanians: Past Glory Reaffirmed

In A.D. 224 the Sasanians, founders of a vigorous new empire, overcame the Parthians, who had been weakened by internal strife and repeated conflicts with Roman legions. In the next four centuries—until they in turn fell before the rising tide of Islam in A.D. 642—the Sasanians reabsorbed the countries of western Asia that had been conquered by Cyrus and Darius, kept Rome and the later Christian Byzantine Empire at bay and furthered the renaissance of Achaemenid traditions begun by Parthians.

The Sasanians not only exalted Zoroastrianism, with its fire cult, as their official religion, but in reliefs like the one below insisted that their own King of Kings had received the diadem of royal power from the Persian god Ahuramazda. But unlike the Achaemenids, who were tolerant of other faiths, the Sasanians were zealous Zoroastrian missionaries, imposing the prophet's creed forcibly upon all their subjects.

Double images of a Sasanian king, Shapur I, guard a stepped fire altar on a gold coin minted in the Third Century A.D. The motif, including the king's crenulated crown and his long sceptre, derives from reliefs carved on Achaemenid tombs near Persepolis.

Ardashir I, Sasanian conqueror of the Parthians, marked his investiture in A.D. 224 in this rock-carved scene. The sovereign (left) accepts a heavy ring—an insignia of kingship—from the god Ahuramazda, represented here as a mounted man instead of a winged spirit. The tableau, nearly 14 feet high, is set in a cliff at Naqsh-i Rustam near the Achaemenids' tombs, some of which bear comparable carvings. Ardashir presumably chose the site both to assert his claim of descent from those kings and to demonstrate that he, too, exercised his rule through the favour of the highest Zoroastrian god.

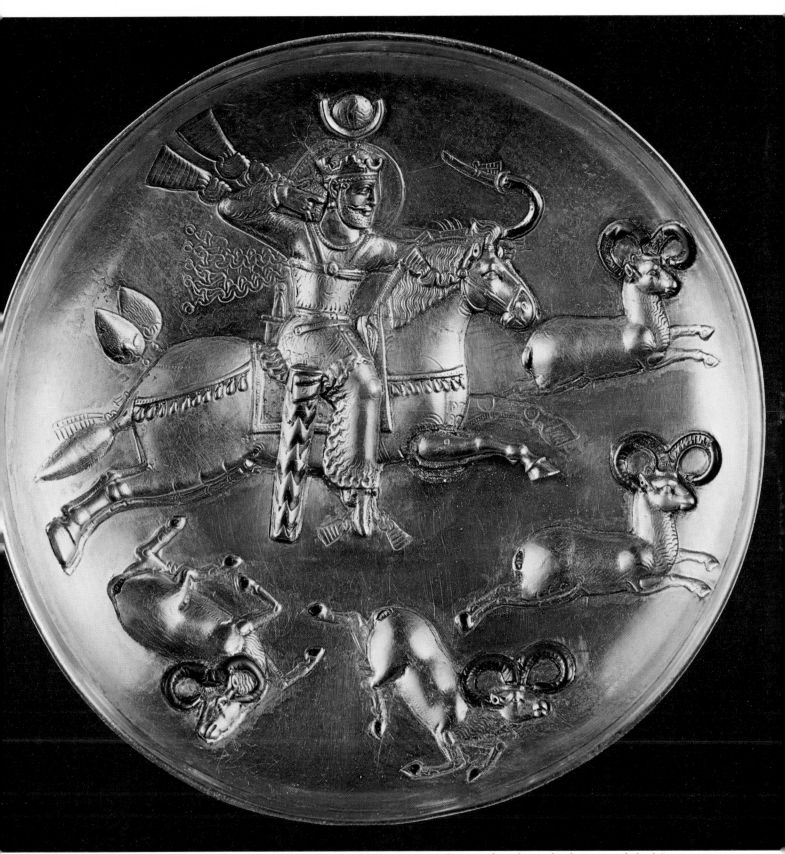

On this gilded silver plate, about eight inches in diameter, a Fifth Century A.D. *Sasanian king hunts the ibex, a symbol of Persian power.*

Defeated in A.D. *260 by the Sasanian Shapur I, two Roman leaders—the emperor Valerian and Philip the Arab (kneeling)—abase themselves bef*

ir conqueror. Shapur's triumph was commemorated in this 25-foot-high stone carving near the sepulchres of similarly victorious Achaemenids.

The Emergence of Man

This chart records the progression of life on earth from its first appearance in the warm waters of the new-formed planet through the evolution of man himself; it traces his physical, social, technological and intellectual development to the Christian era. To place these advances in commonly used chronological sequences, the column at the

Geology	Archaeology	Thousand Millions of Years Ago	
Precambrian earliest era		4.5	Creation of the Earth
		4	Formation of the primordial sea
		3	First life, single-celled algae and bacteria, appears in water
		2	
		1	

		Millions of Years Ago	
			First oxygen-breathing animals appear
		800	
			Primitive organisms develop interdependent specialized cells
		600	Shell-bearing multicelled invertebrate animals appear
Palaeozoic ancient life			Evolution of armoured fish, first animals to possess backbones
		400	Small amphibians venture on to land
			Reptiles and insects arise
			Thecodont, ancestor of dinosaurs, arises
Mesozoic middle life		200	Age of dinosaurs begins
			Birds appear
			Mammals live in shadow of dinosaurs
			Age of dinosaurs ends
		80	
			Prosimians, earliest primates, develop in trees
Cainozoic recent life		60	
		40	Monkeys and apes evolve
		20	
		10	Ramapithecus, oldest known primate with apparently man-like traits, evolves in India and Africa
		8	
		6	Australopithecus, closest primate ancestor to man, appears in Africa
		4	

Geology	Archaeology	Millions of Years Ago	
Lower Pleistocene oldest period of most recent epoch	**Lower Palaeolithic** oldest period of Old Stone Age	2	Oldest known tool fashioned by man in Africa
		1	First true man, Homo erectus, emerges in East Indies and Africa
			Homo erectus populates temperate zone

		Thousands of Years Ago	
Middle Pleistocene middle period of most recent epoch		800	Man learns to control and use fire
		600	
			Large-scale, organized elephant hunts staged in Europe
		400	Man begins to make artificial shelters from branches
		200	
Upper Pleistocene latest period of most recent epoch	**Middle Palaeolithic** middle period of Old Stone Age		Neanderthal man emerges in Europe
		80	
		60	Ritual burials in Europe and Middle East suggest belief in afterlife
			Woolly mammoths hunted by Neanderthal in northern Europe
		40	Cave bear becomes focus of cult in Europe
	Upper Palaeolithic latest period of Old Stone Age		Cro-Magnon man arises in Europe
			Asian hunters cross Bering Land Bridge to populate New World
			Oldest known written record, lunar notations on bone, made in Europe
			Man reaches Australia
			First artists decorate walls and ceilings of caves in France and Spain
		30	Figurines sculpted for nature worship
		20	Invention of needle makes sewing possible
			Bison hunting begins on Great Plains of North America
Holocene present epoch	**Mesolithic** Middle Stone Age	10	Bow and arrow invented in Europe
			Pottery first made in Japan

(Last Ice Age — vertical label in Upper Pleistocene / Upper Palaeolithic section)

▼ Four thousand million years ago   ▼ Three thousand million years ago

▲ Origin of the Earth (4,500 million)   ▲ First life (3,500 million)

eft of each of the chart's four sections identifies the great geo-
cal eras into which the earth's history is divided by scientists,
e the second column lists the archaeological ages of human his-
. The key dates in the rise of life and of man's outstanding
mplishments appear in the third column (years and events mentioned in this volume of The Emergence of Man appear in bold type).
The chart is not to scale; the reason is made clear by the bar below,
which represents in linear scale the 4,500 million years spanned by the
chart—on the scaled bar, the portion relating to the total period of
known human existence (*far right*) is too small to be distinguished.

ology	Archaeology	Years B.C.	
ocene (nt.)	Neolithic New Stone Age	9000	
			Sheep domesticated in Middle East
			Dog domesticated in North America
		8000	Jericho, oldest known city, settled
			Goat domesticated in Persia
			Man cultivates his first crops, wheat and barley, in Middle East
		7000	Pattern of village life grows in Middle East
			Catal Hüyük, in what is now Turkey, becomes largest Neolithic city
			Loom invented in Middle East
			Cattle domesticated in Middle East
		6000	Agriculture begins to replace hunting in Europe
			Copper used in trade in Mediterranean area
	Copper Age		Corn cultivated in Mexico
		4800	Oldest known massive stone monument built in Brittany
		4000	Sail-propelled boats used in Egypt
			First city-states develop in Sumer
			Cylinder seals begin to be used as marks of identification in Middle East
		3500	First potatoes grown in South America
			Wheel originates in Sumer
			Man begins to cultivate rice in Far East
			Silk moth domesticated in China
			Horse domesticated in south Russia
			Egyptian merchant trading ships start to ply the Mediterranean
			Pictograph writing invented in Middle East
	Bronze Age	3000	Bronze first used to make tools in Middle East
			City life spreads to Nile Valley
			Plough is developed in Middle East
			Accurate calendar based on stellar observation devised in Egypt
		2800	Stonehenge, most famous of ancient stone monuments, begun in England
			Pyramids built in Egypt
		2600	Variety of gods and heroes glorified in *Gilgamesh* and other epics in Middle East

Geology	Archaeology	Years B.C.	
Holocene (cont.)	Bronze Age (cont.)	2500	Cities rise in the Indus Valley
			Earliest evidence of use of skis in Scandinavia
			Earliest written code of laws drawn up in Sumer
			Minoan palace societies begin on Crete
		2000	
			Use of bronze in Europe
			Chicken and elephant domesticated in Indus Valley
			Eskimo culture begins in Bering Strait area
		1500	Invention of ocean-going outrigger canoes enables man to reach islands of South Pacific
			Ceremonial bronze sculptures created in China
			Imperial government, ruling distant provinces, established by Hittites
		1400	Iron in use in Middle East
			First complete alphabet devised in script of the Ugarit people in Syria
			Moses leads Israelites out of Egypt
	Iron Age	1000	Reindeer domesticated in Eurasia
			Phoenicians spread alphabet
		900	
		800	Use of iron begins to spread throughout Europe
			First highway system built in Assyria
			Homer composes *Iliad* and *Odyssey*
			Mounted nomads appear in the Middle East as a new and powerful force
			Rome founded
		700	Etruscan civilization in Italy
			Cyrus the Great rules Persian Empire
		500	Roman Republic established
			Wheel barrow invented in China
		200	Epics about India's gods and heroes, the *Mahabharata* and *Ramayana*, written
			Water wheel invented in Middle East
		0	Christian era begins

▼Two thousand million years ago

▼One thousand million years ago

First oxygen-breathing animals (900 million) ▲

First animals to possess ▲
backbones (470 million)

First men (1.3 million) ▲

Credits

The sources for the illustrations in this book are shown below. Credits from left to right are separated by semicolons, from top to bottom by dashes.

All quotations from Herodotus are from *Herodotus, The Histories*, translated by Aubrey de Sélincourt, copyright the Estate of Aubrey de Sélincourt, 1954, reprinted by permission of Penguin Books Ltd.

Cover—Painting by Michael A. Hampshire, background photograph by Antonello Perissinotto. 8—Courtesy of Silvana Editoriale d'Arte and the Archaeological Museum, Tehran. 13—Map by Rafael D. Palacios. 15—Desmond Harney from Robert Harding Associates. 16—James Burke, from the TIME-LIFE Picture Agency. 17—Erwin Böhm courtesy the Archaeological Museum, Tehran. 18—Courtesy The University Museum, University of Pennsylvania. 20—Erwin Böhm courtesy the Archaeological Museum, Tehran—Paulus Leeser courtesy The Metropolitan Museum of Art—Josephine Powell courtesy the Archaeological Museum, Tehran. 22—Drawing from *Monuments de Ninive*, Vol. I, by P. E. Botta and E. Flandin, Paris, 1849, Plate 70. 23—Claus Breede courtesy the Royal Ontario Museum. 24—Courtesy F. Bruckmann K.G., Munich. 27—Erwin Böhm. 29—Professor Heinz Lushey. 30—Derek Bayes courtesy of the Trustees of the British Museum, London; Dr. Werner Dutz. 31—Sybil Sassoon from Robert Harding Associates—Drawing adapted by Nicholas Fasciano from a photograph courtesy the German Archaeological Institute, Tehran. 32—Brian Brake from Rapho Guillumette; Robert Harding. 35—Roland and Sabrina Michaud from Rapho Guillumette. 36, 37—Left, Professor Gerold Walser; Bottom, Courtesy of the Oriental Institute, University of Chicago. 38, 39—Erwin Böhm; Klaus Gallas. 40, 41—Robert Harding; Courtesy of the Oriental Institute, University of Chicago. 42, 43—Professor Gerold Walser; Robert Harding. 44—The Metropolitan Museum of Art, Harris Brisbane Dick Fund, 1954. 48, 49—Courtesy of the Oriental Institute, University of Chicago. 50—The Tourist Photo Library. 52, 53—Olive Kitson courtesy the British Institute of Persian Studies, Tehran; David Stronach courtesy the British Institute of Persian Studies, Tehran. 55—Professor Friedrich Krefter. 56—Roloff Beny courtesy the Archaeological Museum, Tehran. 58—Réunion des Musées Nationaux. 59—Photo Bulloz courtesy Musée du Louvre, Paris. 63 to 69—Drawings by Michael A. Hampshire. 70—C. M. Dixon courtesy of the Trustees of the British Museum, London. 73—Photo Bibliothèque Nationale courtesy of the Cabinet des Médailles, Bibliothèque Nationale, Paris. 75—Dmitri Kessel courtesy Musée du Louvre, Paris. 79—Courtesy of the Trustees of the British Museum, London—Peter Clayton courtesy of the Trustees of the British Museum, London. 80—Henry Groskinsky courtesy Musée du Louvre, Paris; Photo Bibliothèque Nationale, Paris—Courtesy the Foroughi Collection. 81—Jack Escaloni courtesy of the Trustees of the British Museum, London—Courtesy Musée du Louvre, Paris. 85—Antikenabteilung, Staatliche Museen zu Berlin. 86—Dmitri Kessel courtesy Musée du Louvre, Paris; The Metropolitan Museum of Art, Rogers Fund, 1954. 87—Courtesy of the Trustees of the British Museum, London—Courtesy of the Oriental Institute, University of Chicago. 88—Private Collection, Paris. 89—Courtesy the Iran Bastan Museum, Tehran—William MacQuitty courtesy the Archaeological Museum, Tehran. 90—C. M. Dixon courtesy of the Trustees of the British Museum, London; The Metropolitan Museum of Art, Harris Brisbane Dick Fund, 1954. 91—Courtesy of the Trustees of the British Museum, London. 92—William MacQuitty. 95—Courtesy of Silvana Editoriale d'Arte and the Foroughi Collection. 97—David Stronach courtesy the British Institute of Persian Studies, Tehran. 98—YANKI News Magazine Picture Service courtesy Topkapi Museum, Istanbul. 100—David Stronach courtesy the British Institute of Persian Studies, Tehran. 102—Bury Peerless. 103—Jehangir Gazdar. 104—Josephine Powell. 106—William MacQuitty. 108, 109—Paulus Leeser courtesy Rare Book Division, The New York Public Library, Astor, Lenox and Tilden Foundations. 112—Klaus Gallas. 114, 115—Erwin Böhm. 116—Courtesy of the Oriental Institute, University of Chicago. 118—Robert Harding—Roger Wood. 119—Dr. Werner Dutz. 123—Courtesy of the Oriental Institute, University of Chicago. 125—Klaus Gallas. 126, 127—William MacQuitty; Professor Friedrich Krefter. 128, 129—William MacQuitty—Professor Friedrich Krefter. 130, 131—Erwin Böhm; Professor Friedrich Krefter. 132—YANKI News Magazine Picture Service courtesy Topkapi Museum, Istanbul. 136—Courtesy F. Bruckmann K.G., Munich. 138, 139—Robert Harding. 141—Peter Davey courtesy of the Trustees of the British Museum, London. 142, 143—Scala courtesy Museo Nazionale, Naples. 147—Bill Ray, from the TIME-LIFE Picture Agency. 148—Courtesy Yale University—Peter Davey courtesy of the Trustees of the British Museum, London. 149—Erwin Böhm. 150—Photo Bibliothèque Nationale courtesy of the Cabinet des Médailles, Bibliothèque Nationale, Paris—Erwin Böhm. 151—The Metropolitan Museum of Art, Fletcher Fund, 1934. 152, 153—Erwin Böhm.

Acknowledgments

For the help given in the preparation of this book, the editors are particularly indebted to Carl Nylander, Associate Professor, Department of Classical and Near Eastern Archaeology, Bryn Mawr College, Bryn Mawr, Pennsylvania. The editors also wish to express their gratitude to Zeren Akalay, Topkapi Museum, Istanbul; Pierre Amiet, Chief Curator, Department of Oriental Antiquities, Louvre Museum, Paris; Nosratullah Ayeli, Director General of Public Relations Office, Ministry of Culture and Arts, Tehran; Firooz Bagherzadeh, Director of Iran Bastan Museum, Tehran; Farnaz Bahmanyar, Iran Bastan Museum, Tehran; Catherine Bélanger, Photographic Service, Louvre Museum, Paris; Filiz Cagman, Topkapi Museum, Istanbul; George G. Cameron, Professor, Department of Near Eastern Studies, University of Michigan, Ann Arbor; Annie Caubet, Curator, Department of Oriental Antiquities, Louvre Museum, Paris; Raoul Curiel, Cabinet des Médailles, Bibliothèque Nationale, Paris; Robert H. Dyson Jr., Professor of Anthropology and Curator of the Near East Section, The University Museum, University of Pennsylvania, Philadelphia; Editions Gallimard-L'Univers des Formes, Paris; Ann E. Farkas, New York City; Roman Ghirshman, Paris; Theresa Goell, Director, Nemrud Dagh Excavations, New York City; Clare Goff, Scrooby, Yorkshire, England; Barbara Grunwald, the German Archaeological Institute, Tehran; Prudence Oliver Harper, Curator, Department of Ancient Near Eastern Art, The Metropolitan Museum of Art, New York City; Michael Ingraham, Research Assistant, Near East Section, The University Museum, University of Pennsylvania, Philadelphia; Professor Friedrich Krefter, Rhöndorf, Germany; Louis D. Levine, Associate Curator, West Asian Department, Royal Ontario Museum, Toronto, Canada; Professor Heinz Lushey, Tübingen, Germany; Mohammed Matin, Press Counsellor, Iranian Embassy, Ankara, Turkey; T. C. Mitchell, Department of Western Asiatic Antiquities, British Museum, London; Ezatullah Negahban, Professor of Archaeology and Dean of Archaeological Department, University of Tehran; Enrica Pozzi, Director, National Archaeological Museum, Naples; M. J. Price, Department of Coins and Medals, British Museum, London; Aziz Rashki, Tehran; Umberto Scerrato, I.S. M.E.O., Rome; David Stronach, Director of the British Institute of Persian Studies, Tehran; Françoise Tallon, Researcher, Department of Oriental Antiquities, Louvre Museum, Paris; Edward Telesford, Photographic Service, British Museum, London; Maurizio Tosi, I.S.M.E.O., Rome; Giuseppe Tucci, President, I.S.M.E.O., Rome; Hubertus von Gall, the German Archaeological Institute, Tehran; Nancy M. Waggoner, Associate Curator of Greek Coins, American Numismatic Society, New York City.

Bibliography

*Denotes published in US only.

Bengtson, Hermann, ed., *The Greeks and Persians*. Translated from the German by J. Conway. Weidenfeld and Nicolson, 1969.

Burn, A. R., *Persia and the Greeks*. Edward Arnold, 1962.

Burns, Arthur F., *Money and Monetary Policy in Early Times*. Kelley, USA, 1970.

Bury, J. B., S. A. Cook and F. E. Adcock, eds., *The Cambridge Ancient History*, Vol. IV, *The Persian Empire and the West*. Cambridge University Press, 1969.

Cameron, George C., *History of Early Iran*. The University of Chicago Press, 1969.

Casson, Lionel, *The Ancient Mariners*. Gollancz, 1959.

Cowley, Arthur, *Aramaic Papyri of the Fifth Century B.C.* Oxford University Press, 1923. (Now out of print).

*Culican, William, *The Medes and Persians*. Frederick A. Praeger, 1965.

Driver, G. R., *Aramaic Documents of the Fifth Century B.C.* Oxford University Press, 1957.

*Dyson, Robert H., Jr., "Problems of Proto-historic Iran As Seen from Hasanlu." *Journal of Near Eastern Studies*. Vol. XXIV, *Persian Art: The Parthian and Sasanian*

*Forbes, R. J., *Man the Maker: A History of Technology and Engineering*. Abelard-Schuman, 1958.
Studies in Ancient Technology. Vols. I, II, IV. E. G. Brill, 1965.

Frankfort, Henri, *The Art and Architecture of the Ancient Orient*. Penguin Books, 1970.

*Frye, Richard N., *The Heritage of Persia*. The World Publishing Company, 1963.

*Ghirshman, Roman, *The Arts of Ancient Iran: From Its Origins to the Time of Alexander the Great*. Translated from the French by Stuart Gilbert and James Emmons. Golden Press, 1964.
Iran. Penguin Books, 1954. (Now out of print).
Persian Art: The Parthian and Sassanian Dynasties. Translated from the French by Stuart Gilbert and James Emmons. Golden Press, 1962.

*Godard, André, *The Art of Iran*. Frederick A. Praeger, 1965.

*Goell, Theresa and F. K. Doerner, "The Tomb of Antiochus I". *Scientific American*. July, 1956.

*Henning, W. B., "The Monuments and Inscriptions of Tang-i-Sarvak". *Asia Major*. New Series, Vol. II, Part 2, 1952.

Herodotus, *The Histories*. Translated from the Greek by Aubrey de Selincourt. Penguin Books, 1971.

Hinnells, John R., *Persian Mythology*. The Hamlyn Publishing Group Limited, 1973.

*Kent, Roland G., *Old Persian Grammar Texts Lexicon*. American Oriental Society, 1953.

*Krefter, Friedrich, *Persepolis Rekonstruktionen*. Gebr. Mann Verlag, 1971.

*Levine, Louis D., "Of Medes and Media". *Rotunda*. The Bulletin of the Royal Ontario Museum, Vol. 3, No. 1. Winter 1970.

*Lukonin, Vladimir G., *Persia II*. Translated from the Russian by James Hogarth. Nagel Publishers, 1967.

Mallowan, Max, "Cyrus the Great". *Iran*. Vol. X. The British Institute of Persian Studies, 1972.

Matheson, Sylvia A., *Persia: An Archaeological Guide*. Faber, 1972.

Mellaart, James, *Earliest Civilizations of the Near East*. Thames and Hudson, 1965.

*Muscarella, Oscar W., *The Metropolitan Museum of Art Bulletin*. Vol. XXV, No. 3, November, 1966.

The New English Bible. Oxford University Press and Cambridge University Press, 1970.

Noss, John B., *Man's Religions*. Collier-Macmillan, 1969.

Nylander, Carl, *Ionians in Pasargadae: Studies in Old Persian Architecture*. Almqvist, 1971. (Swedish Publisher).

Olmstead, Albert ten Eyck, *History of the Persian Empire*. University of Chicago Press, 1948.

*Pannekoek, A., *A History of Astronomy*. Interscience Publishers, Inc., 1961.

*Porada, Edith, *The Art of Ancient Iran: Pre-Islamic Cultures*. Crown Publishers Inc., 1962.

Pritchard, James B., *The Ancient Near East in Pictures Relating to the Old Testament*. Princeton University Press, 1970.
Ancient Near Eastern Texts Relating to the Old Testament. Princeton University Press, 1970.

*Pudney, John, *Suez: De Lesseps' Canal*. Frederick A. Praeger, 1968.

*Rostovzeff, Michael I., "Dura and the Problem of Parthian Art". *Yale Classical Studies*. Vol. V, 1935.

*Schmidt, Erich F.:
Persepolis I: Structures, Reliefs, Inscriptions. The University of Chicago Oriental Institute Publications. The University of Chicago Press, 1953.

* *Persepolis II: Contents of the Treasury and Other Discoveries*. The University of Chicago Oriental Institute Publications. The University of Chicago Press, 1957.
Persepolis III: The Royal and Other Monuments. The University of Chicago Oriental Institute Publications. The University of Chicago Press, 1971.

*Schreiber, Hermann, *Merchants, Pilgrims and Highwaymen*. G. P. Putnam's Sons, 1962.

*Siegfried, André, *Suez and Panama*. Harcourt, Brace and Company, 1940.

Singer, Charles E. G. Holmyard, A. R. Hall and Trevor I. Williams, eds., *A History of Technology*. Vols. I, II. Oxford University Press, 1954.

Strabo, *The Geography*. Vol. 7, Loeb Classical Library. Heinemann, 1930.

Stronach, David, "Excavations at Tepe Nush-i Jan. 1967". *Iran*. Journal of the British Institute of Persian Studies. The British Academy, Burlington House, 1969.

*Wilber, Donald N., *Persepolis, The Archaeology of Parsa, Seat of the Persian Kings*. Thomas Y. Crowell Company, 1969.

Wilson, Arnold T., *The Suez Canal: Its Past, Present and Future*. Oxford University Press, 1939. (Now out of print).

Wiseman, D. J., *Peoples of the Old Testament*. Oxford University Press, 1973.

*Wiseman, D. J. and W. and B. Forman, *Cylinder Seals of Western Asia*. Batchworth Press.

Xenophon:
Cyropaedia. Loeb Classical Library. Heinemann, 1914.
Memorabilia and Oeconomicus. Translated from the Greek by E. C. Marchant. Loeb Classical Library. Heinemann, 1923.

*Young, T. Guyler, Jr., *Excavations at Godin Tepe: First Progress Report*. Royal Ontario Museum, 1969.

*Young, T. Guyler, Jr., and Louis D. Levine, *Excavations of the Godin Project: Second Progress Report*. Royal Ontario Museum, 1974.

Zaehner, R. C., *The Dawn and Twilight of Zoroastrianism*. Weidenfeld and Nicolson, 1961. (Now out of print).

Index

Numerals in italics indicate an illustration of the subject mentioned.

Filmsetting by C. E. Dawkins (Typesetters) Ltd., London, SE1 1UN
Printed and bound in Belgium by Brepols Fabrieken N.V.